A LIFE OF
JOSEPH PRIESTLEY

Joseph Priestley.

A LIFE OF
JOSEPH PRIESTLEY

By ANNE HOLT

With an Introduction by
FRANCIS W. HIRST

GREENWOOD PRESS, PUBLISHERS
WESTPORT, CONNECTICUT

Originally published in 1931
by Oxford University Press, London

First Greenwood Reprinting 1970

Library of Congress Catalogue Card Number 75-109750

SBN 8371-4240-7

Printed in the United States of America

PREFACE

JOSEPH PRIESTLEY, whose name was a household word among his contemporaries, is now scarcely remembered outside the circles of the scientist and historian. This fate is partially due to the inadequacy of the existing biographies, but also to the general preference of the public for the lives of the notorious over those of the brave and industrious. As a scientist Priestley has fared less hardly than as a philosopher, politician, theologian, and historian, for his biography was written for the English Men of Science series by Sir Edward Thorpe. But this excellent, though slight, Life is naturally most concerned with Priestley's scientific work, and his other activities are merely outlined. Most important biographically is Rutt's Life, which is a mine of information consisting of Priestley's own Memoirs with a continuation by his son Joseph, to which is added much of his correspondence. Many of these letters are in Dr. Williams's Library, where, by the courtesy of the Librarian, I have been able to see them. Rutt cannot be said to have followed slavishly the originals either in his reprint of the Memoirs or in his transcription of the letters. In fact, in the latter he has omitted where he liked without any warning, and in one place at least, with extracts from two letters he has made one. Rutt has made no contribution to the Life beyond adding voluminous notes.

It was thus with the object of rescuing from oblivion Priestley's many-sided life that this study was undertaken. It is quite impossible to thank all those who have helped and encouraged me. To the descendants of Priestley, both here and in America, I am greatly indebted, and take this opportunity of thanking Mrs. Belloc-Lowndes for lending me papers in her possession, and Mr. Joseph Priestley Button of Chestnut Hill, Pa., for the use of letters, and for allowing me to reproduce the portrait by Peale as frontispiece. Mrs. William Forsyth, who took me to Northumberland, has not, alas, lived to see the book in which she showed so much interest.

I have also to thank the Marquis of Lansdowne for the loan of papers from his collection at Bowood. Dr. Frederick Griffin not only lent me papers in possession of the First Unitarian Church, Philadelphia, but was also the means of my coming at many more. Mr. A. C. Egerton, F.R.S., has helped me with expert advice on the chapter dealing with Priestley's scientific work, and the Rev. Lawrence Redfern with that on Metaphysics, but they are not to be held responsible for the views I have expressed. Miss Robina Addis has provided the index, and Mrs. Margaret Locket has read the proofs. To all of these I am deeply grateful.

CONTENTS

INTRODUCTION
by FRANCIS W. HIRST

IT was high time that an adequate biography of Joseph Priestley, embodying information which escaped contemporary writers and enlightened by scientific criticism, should be written to revive the fame of an almost forgotten eighteenth-century Worthy, who united empiricism in science with rationalism in theology and helped to found a new school of philosophic radicalism. Miss Holt has performed this service in an admirable book which needs no introduction; but being called in to execute an act of supererogation I can plead two excuses—the first that I have always been an admirer of Priestley, and the second that, having persuaded the author to become his biographer, I could not well deny her request that I should furnish a foreword.

Joseph Priestley's birthplace was within easy ride of mine, and I am familiar from boyhood with the scenery and life of the woollen district of the West Riding where he was brought up. It has nursed innumerable men of invention and industry who, by their natural talents and indomitable energy, have developed and enriched during the last two centuries one of the greatest manufacturing districts in the world. Independence of mind, a born love of controversy, and a relish for telling unpalatable truths both in private and public life, are well-known characteristics of the shire. Priestley, the son of a Leeds clothier, might have been born to exemplify all the traits and talents of the typical Yorkshireman. His versatility reminds us of the Greek in Juvenal, of the Frenchman in Johnson's *London*, or of Dryden's Zimri:

> A man so various that he seemed to be
> Not one but all mankind's epitome.

But in Priestley's versatility there was no trace of pliability. So far from betraying weakness, his character combined an unusual obstinacy of opinion and a strong moral purpose with a progressive but consistent faith, a love of righteousness and a love of truth. Indeed, the text which his friend Thomas Jefferson chose as motto for the University of Virginia might well have been engraven on Priestley's crest, as it was the hall-mark and glory of Priestley's life:

'Ye shall know the truth and the truth shall make you free.'

It may be, as Miss Holt suggests, that the diversity of Priestley's interests debarred him from attaining that pinnacle of greatness on which some of his contemporaries and friends, or acquaintances, like Adam Smith, Edmund Burke, Benjamin Franklin, Washington, Jefferson, and Turgot, are securely seated. One who aspired to be preacher and teacher, linguist and historian, grammarian and flute-player, chemist and theologian, was hardly likely to achieve the highest success in all or any of these callings. But if his energies were dissipated in too many directions, his speculations were not fruitless. In the provinces of metaphysics and theology, he made a useful mark, if not an indelible imprint, on liberal and progressive thought. In the eyes of the intolerant and the narrow-minded he was an atheist, though he believed in God, and an infidel, though he gloried in the gospel and anticipated the Second Coming. His faith or credulity extended even to the Book of Daniel; and towards the end of his life, after the first victories of Napoleon, he confidently expected the 'downfall of all the states represented by the ten toes in the image of Nebuchadnezzar and the ten horns of the fourth beast of Daniel, before the present war be over'.

A stalwart Nonconformist all his life, he passed from the Independents to the Unitarians; a life-long opponent and critic of State establishments, he represented alike in controversy and in action the dissidence of dissent and the protestantism of the protestant religion. Those who have dipped into his polemical writings will agree that, if he had paid some attention to style, they would be less voluminous and more readable. It will also be admitted that, if he had acquired a *suaviter in modo* as well as a *fortiter in re,* they would be more pleasant and persuasive. But these are blemishes which he shares with many scientists and theologians, who possessed neither his originality nor his moral courage.

Priestley's martyrdom was worthy of the Age of Reason. He was punished for political and religious heresy not by 'lifted axe' or 'agonising wheel', but by the destruction of his laboratory and library. Thus a romantic halo was thrown round his career. The martyr became an exile. The friend of Benjamin Franklin in England became the friend of Thomas Jefferson in the United States. A Fellow of the Royal Society was driven to take refuge in a new republic which had rejected royalty. Fortunately Priestley's democratic liberalism blended easily with the régime of liberal republicanism and toleration inaugurated by Jefferson. Jeremy Bentham himself could not have devised a constitution, or chosen a President, better suited to Priestley's temperament, or a home more befitting the declining years of one who had fought so hard for radicalism in politics and Unitarianism in religion. But ours is an age of science and mechanics rather than of doctrine; and I fear it may be true that, until idealism returns, Priestley's fame will depend not so much upon his character and philosophy as upon his discovery of oxygen and his invention of champagne or soda-water.

BIBLIOGRAPHY AND MANUSCRIPT SOURCES, WITH ABBREVIATIONS

Adams, *Works* = Works of John Adams, 2nd President of the United States. 1856.

Air = Joseph Priestley. Experiments and Observations on different Kinds of Air, in three volumes, being the former six volumes abridged and methodized, with many additions. 1791. (These volumes do not include the Prefaces which appeared in the original volumes.)

Alger, J. G. English Men in the French Revolution. 1889.

Am. Philos. Soc. MSS. = Original Letters in the possession of the American Philosophical Society at Philadelphia.

Appeal to the Public = Joseph Priestley. Appeal to the Public on the Subject of the Riots in Birmingham. 2nd edition, 1792.

Belloc-Lowndes MSS. = Original Letters in the possession of Mrs. Belloc-Lowndes.

Belsham = Thomas Belsham. Memoir of the Rev. Theophilus Lindsey, M.A. Centenary Edition. 1873.

Blackburne, *Works* = Francis Blackburne. Works, Theological and Miscellaneous. 1805.

Bowood MSS. = Original Letters in the possession of the Marquis of Lansdowne at Bowood.

Brett, G. S. History of Psychology. 1912.

Bright, Henry A. Historical Sketch of Warrington Academy. 1859. Reprinted from Transactions of the Historic Society of Lancashire and Cheshire 1858-9.

Brown, *Fr. Revolution* = Philip Anthony Brown, M.A. French Revolution in English History. 1918.

Burton, E. H. Life and Times of Bishop Challoner. 1909.

Calamy = S. Palmer. The Nonconformists' Memorial, being an Account of the Ministers who were ejected or silenced after the Restoration, originally written by the Rev. and Learned Edmund Calamy, now abridged and corrected. 1777.

Christian Reformer. May 1835.

Collection of Letters to and from Dr. Priestley, 26 March 1789 to 19 June 1802. Typewritten copies in the British Museum.

Contemporary Review. October 1894.

Corruptions of Christianity = Joseph Priestley. History of the Corruptions of Christianity. 1871 edition.

Crabb Robinson = Thomas Sadler. Diary, Reminiscences, and Correspondence of H. Crabb Robinson. 1869.

Dale, B. Yorkshire Puritanism and Early Noncomformity. 1917.

Darwin, Charles. *Erasmus Darwin* = Ernest Krause. Erasmus Darwin, with preliminary notice by Charles Darwin. 1879.

Defoe. *Tour* = Daniel Defoe. A Tour through the whole Island of Great Britain. 3rd edition, 1742; and 1927 edition.

D.N.B. = Dictionary of National Biography.

Disquisitions = Joseph Priestley, Disquisitions relating to Matter and Spirit. 2nd edition, 1782.

Doctrine of Phlogiston = Joseph Priestley. Doctrine of Phlogiston Established. 1783.

Edgeworth, *Memoirs* = Memoirs of Richard Lovell Edgeworth Esq., by himself. 2nd edition, 1822.

Electricity = Joseph Priestley. History of Electricity. 2nd edition, 1769.

Enfield, William. Remarks on several late Publications relative to the Dissenters in a *Letter to Dr. Priestley*. 1770.

Faujas de Saint-Fond = Barthelemi Faujas de Saint-Fond. Travels in England, Scotland, and the Hebrides. 1799.

Fitzmaurice = Lord Fitzmaurice. Life of William, Earl of Shelburne, afterwards first Marquis of Lansdowne. 2nd edition, 1912.

Field, *Life of Parr* = William Field. Memoirs of the Life, Writings and Opinions of the Rev. Samuel Parr, LL.D. 1828.

Furness. *Sermon* = William Henry Furness, D.D. Recollections of Seventy Years. A discourse delivered in the First Unitarian Church in Philadelphia.

Gilchrist, A. Life of Blake. 1880.

Gordon, Alexander. Heads of Unitarian Church History with appended lectures on Baxter and Priestley. 1895.

Gordon, Alexander. Cheshire Classis Minutes. 1919.

Hartley = David Hartley. Observations on Man. 1791 edition.

Henry, William. Estimate of the Philosophical Character of Dr. Priestley. 1832.

Horne Tooke Notes = Marginal Notes by Horne Tooke in the British Museum copy of 1st edition of the *Disquisitions*. 1777.

Horsley, *Tracts* = Samuel Horsley, D.D. Tracts in controversy with Priestley. 1789.

James, William. Some Problems of Philosophy. 1911.

Knox, H. V. Will to be Free. 1928.

Langford = J. A. Langford. A Century of Birmingham Life. 1868.

Lectures on History = Joseph Priestley. Lectures on History and General Policy; to which is prefixed an Essay on a Course of Education for Civil and Active Life. 1840 edition, with notes by Rutt unless otherwise stated.

Letters to Burke = Joseph Priestley. Letters to the Right Honourable Edmund Burke occasioned by his Reflections on the Revolution in France. 3rd edition, 1791.

Letters to a Philosophic Unbeliever = Joseph Priestley. Letters to a Philosophic Unbeliever. 2nd edition, 1787.

Library of Congress MSS. = Letters in the possession of the Library of Congress, Washington.

Mass. Hist. Soc. MSS. = Letters in the possession of the Massachusetts Historical Society at Boston.

Memoirs = Memoirs of Dr. Joseph Priestley, to the year 1795, written by himself; with a continuation to the time of his decease, by his son Joseph Priestley. 1806.

Meteyard = Eliza Meteyard. Life of Josiah Wedgwood. 1865.

Monthly Repository. 1806–26; 1827–37.

Morellet = Lettres de l'Abbé Morellet à Lord Shelburne. 1898.

Morison = S. E. Morison. The Oxford History of the United States. 1927.

Orton Letters = Rev. Job Orton. Letters to Dissenting Ministers and Students. 1806.

Parker = Irene Parker. Dissenting Academies in England. 1914.

Peel, Frank. Nonconformity in Spen Valley. 1891.

Pa. Hist. Soc. MSS. = Letters in the possession of the Historical Society of Pennsylvania, at Philadelphia.

Priestley's *Hartley* = Joseph Priestley. Hartley's Theory of the Human Mind, on the Principle of the Association of Ideas, with Essays relating to the subject. 1777.

Priestley, Timothy. Funeral Sermons occasioned by the Death of the late Rev. Joseph Priestley. 1804.

Randall, *The Wilkinsons* = John Randall. Our Coal and Iron Industries and the men who have wrought in connexion with them. The Wilkinsons. 1879.

Rogers, *Table Talk* = Alexander Dyce. Table Talk of Samuel Rogers. 1887.

Early Life of Samuel Rogers by P. W. Clayden. 1887.

Royal Society MSS. = Collection of papers relating to Priestley in the Library of the Royal Society.

Russell, *Fox.* Lord John Russell. Life and Times of Charles James Fox. 1859.

Russells of Birmingham = S. H. Jeyes. The Russells of Birmingham in the French Revolution and in America. 1911.

Rutt = J. T. Rutt. Life and Correspondence of Joseph Priestley, LL.D., F.R.S. 1832.

Schimmelpenninck = C. C. Hankin. Life of Mary Anne Schimmelpenninck. 1858.

Schroeder, Rev. L. Mill Hill Chapel.

Scientific Correspondence = H. Carrington Bolton. Scientific Correspondence. (Appendix II is an account of the Lunar Society.)

Seward, A. Memoirs of the Life of Dr. Darwin. 1804.

Smiles = Samuel Smiles. Lives of Boulton and Watt. 1865.

Smith, Ernest Fahls. Priestley in America.

Taylor, John, D.D. of Norwich. Defence of Common Rights of Christians. 3rd edition 1766.

— Principles and Pursuits of an English Presbyterian Minister. 1843.

Theological Repository. 1769–71 and 1784–8.

Thomas = Roland Thomas. Richard Price. 1924.

Thorpe = T. E. Thorpe. Joseph Priestley. English Men of Science Series. 1906.

Turner, W. Lives of Eminent Unitarians. 1840–3.

Wansey = Henry Wansey. Excursion to the United States of America. 2nd edition, 1798.

Wicksteed, Charles. Lectures on the Memory of the Just. 1849.

Dr. Williams' Library MSS. = Letters in the possession of Dr. Williams' Library.

Works = Theological and Miscellaneous Works of Joseph Priestley, edited by J. T. Rutt. 1817–31.

Young, *Travels* = Arthur Young. Travels in France 1787, 1788, 1789, edited Betham Edwards. 4th edition.

CHAPTER I

1733–55

WHEN Defoe travelled through England about 1725 he found it impossible to make a survey in one journey of so large and wealthy a division as the West Riding of Yorkshire, one of 'those remote parts of the North' which are 'the most populous places in Great Britain'.[1] For hundreds of years it had been an important centre of the woollen industry. Here wool brought from other parts of England was woven into all kinds of cloth, and sold at Leeds, Halifax, Bradford, and other market towns for shipment to all corners of the earth, to the American colonies, to Russia, to central Europe as well as for use at home in England. Many of the narrow valleys enclosed by bleak hills, which caused Defoe to complain that his journey consisted of mounting to the clouds, and descending to the water-level, were already busy hives of industry; but those natural beauties had not yet been disfigured, which can still be realized to-day, even though spinning-wheels and handlooms have given way to factories, and country lanes to paved streets.

The independence of Yorkshire men is a commonplace. During the Civil War the sympathies of the West Riding lay with the Parliament; from here many went forth to serve under the Fairfaxes and other local leaders; here both Presbyterianism and Independency took root. In the troubled times which followed the Restoration the ejected ministers travelled from village to village attending to the needs of their flocks. Sometimes they were compelled to hold their services at dead of night and always were they forced to take precautions against the hated informer; often they were persecuted, often imprisoned.

[1] Defoe, *Tour*, 3rd ed., iii. 128.

In the brief period of toleration that followed Charles II's Declaration of Indulgence in 1672, over 120 licences for conventicles were issued in Yorkshire,[1] and though, for the most part, services were held in private houses, some of the older chapels date from this period. But the indulgence was shortlived, and toleration only really began in 1688. Though allowed to worship in their own way, during the whole of the eighteenth century Dissenters were under civil disabilities: thus religion, always the centre of the Puritan's life, became through restrictive legislation one of the few ways in which he could employ his talents in the service of mankind.

The Priestleys, a large Yorkshire family, were a typical product of the West Riding. At Fieldhead, a little way out of Birstall, already famous in Defoe's time for its dyeing, they had lived for several generations, when Joseph Priestley was born there on March 13th, 1733 (O.S.). 'The house', so Madame Belloc wrote in the *Contemporary Review*, 'is now taken down, but I visited it in my youth, and made a rough sketch, which shows that it was smaller than the house of Shakespeare's birth at Stratford-on-Avon, but of much the same type, and probably very ancient.'[2] His grandfather, another Joseph Priestley, had carried on the business of a maker and dresser of cloth, a man of saintly life, who, on his deathbed, 'sent for nearly thirty of his workmen, and giving them an affectionate exhortation said, "See how a man of God dies", and laid down his head and departed immediately.' Of more remote ancestors we know nothing. Probably they were parliament men, but we can only surmise what stories would be told the young Joseph Priestley, of friends and relations who had stood firm for

---

[1] Dale, *Yorkshire Puritanism and Early Nonconformity.*
[2] *Contemporary Review*, Oct. 1894.

the Commonwealth or who had suffered at the Restoration, what tales of martyrdom in freedom's cause reached his boyish ears, and what memories would come to him in the future, when he too had suffered 'in a good cause with patience'.[1]

In the memoir [2] he wrote for his children, Priestley says that his father was Jonas Priestley, another finisher of cloth, and his mother was the daughter of a farmer called Swift, from Shafton near Wakefield. Joseph was the eldest of six children. Of his mother he remembered little, as he spent most of his early years at his maternal grandfather's.

'I remember, however, that she was careful to teach me the Assembly's Catechism, and to give me the best instructions the little time I was at home. Once in particular, when I was playing with a pin, she asked me where I got it; and on telling her that I found it at my uncle's, who lived very near to my father, and where I had been playing with my cousins, she made me carry it back again; no doubt to impress my mind, as it could not fail to do, with a clear idea of the distinction of property, and the importance of attending to it.[3] She died in the hard winter of 1739, not long after being delivered of my youngest brother; and having dreamed a little before her death that she was in a delightful place, which she particularly described, and imagined to be heaven, the last words she spake, as my aunt informed me, were "let me go to that fine place".'

Joseph was brought home from his grandfather's, where his place was taken by a younger child, but in 1742

[1] *Works*, xxii. 455.
[2] Unless otherwise stated quotations are from the memoir.
[3] Cf. Crabb Robinson's Memoirs for an almost identical story.

he was adopted by his father's sister, Mrs. Keighley, who, until her death in 1764, was in every way a parent to him.

The Keighleys were people of substance living at Heckmondwycke, three miles away from the Priestleys. Their house, the Old Hall, is still standing, though part has been destroyed to make way for a railway cutting, and what is left has been divided into three cottages. Mr. Keighley is reported to have been in his youth a persecutor of Dissenters.

'He sought out the places and times of their meeting for public worship, in order that he might render them amenable to the civil power. Once he determined to secrete himself in one of their places of worship, with a view to detecting their plots, and of exposing their heresies and of consigning them to the vengeance of the law; but like St. Paul, he who went in a persecutor, came out a convert. He heard all that passed, but instead of delivering the minister up to punishment, he took him to his own house, and supported him, till the iron arm of intolerance was broken, and people were allowed to worship the God of their Fathers according to the dictates of their own conscience.'[1]

Soon after Priestley went to live at the Old Hall, Keighley died, leaving the bulk of his property to his widow, 'who knew no other use of wealth, or of talents of any kind, than to do good, and who never spared herself for this purpose'. Her house was a centre of nonconformity, and a 'resort of all the dissenting ministers in the neighbourhood without distinction, and those who were the most obnoxious on account of their heresy were almost as welcome to her, if she thought them honest and good men (which she was not unwilling to do), as any

[1] *The Universal Theological Magazine*, April 1804.

others'. Here Joseph often heard discussed various
theological questions, and probably Whig politics, but
it is only of religion he speaks in his memoir, for in dissenting England two hundred years ago religion was the
first occupation in life. Joseph had learnt the Catechism
at his mother's knee, and Timothy Priestley relates that
his brother at the age of six would ask him to pray with
him. Twice a day Mrs. Keighley prayed with her family,
and after he was grown up the duty fell to Joseph. But
the centre of their religious life was the Independent
Chapel near by.

Even in the worst days of persecution Heckmondwycke
had its small conventicle, and in the period which followed
the Revolution a chapel was built on the hill above the
Old Hall. Several chapels have stood on the same spot,
and to-day there is a modern Congregational church. The
old graveyard still exists round it where lie buried Mrs.
Keighley and many others of the Priestley family. The
chapel no doubt was like others of the period, a simple
meeting-house where it was possible to worship in spirit
and truth 'Him who filleth heaven and earth'. When the
congregation outgrew it, and it became inconvenient,
another was built on the site. Here, Priestley tells us, the
business of religion was efficiently attended to.

'We were all catechized in public till we were grown
up, servants as well as others: the minister always
expounded the scriptures with as much regularity as he
preached, and there was hardly a day in the week in
which there was not some meeting of one part of the
congregation. On one evening there was a meeting of
the young men for conversation and prayer. This I
constantly attended, praying extempore with others
when called upon. At my Aunt's there was a monthly
meeting of women, who acquitted themselves in

prayer as well as any men belonging to the congregation. Being at first a child in the family, I was permitted to attend their meetings, and growing up insensibly, heard them after I was capable of judging.'

Sunday was kept with particular strictness. No one 'was permitted to walk out for recreation, but the whole of the day was spent at the public meeting, or at home in reading, meditation, and prayer, in the family or the closet'. Some of the congregation came from long distances, as did the Priestleys from Fieldhead.

'The services then were invariably in the morning and afternoon, and those who came long distances did not usually return to the midday meal; in fact that was in most cases an impossibility. It was customary for some of them to come on their stout horses with their wives riding behind on the pillion, wheeled vehicles being at that time little used. The animals were put up at the neighbouring hostelry, the "Wool Pack", and in the intervals between the services their owners and their families also went there to refresh themselves. The pastor, too, often joined this little company at dinner, as is evident from the frequent entries in the old church book of charges for "pastor's refreshment".'[1]

Perhaps the rest of the Priestleys went back with the Keighleys, to their cold meal, for on that day no victuals were dressed in any family. Priestley never depreciated his early religious training and has recorded 'that the person to whom, in this world, I have been under the greatest obligation, was at the same time a strict Calvinist, and in all respects as perfect a human character as I have yet been acquainted with'.[2]

[1] Frank Peel, *Nonconformity in Spen Valley*, p. 86.
[2] *Disquisitions*, ii. 199.

In such a home Priestley's upbringing was naturally austere. In later life he wrote that the horror he felt on hearing an oath, or the profane use of the name of God, was so strong that it seemed almost instinctive.[1] Of amusements he relates little except that *Robinson Crusoe* was the only romance that he read before going to the Academy. His brother remembered that he spent most of his time for recreation in reading and study. Mrs. Keighley sent him to several schools in the neighbourhood, 'especially to a large free school' which is supposed to be that at Batley, but where, unfortunately, no register of scholars was kept. Here Priestley learnt Greek and Latin and, during holidays, Hebrew from Mr. Kirkby, the minister at Heckmondwycke. His early fondness for books led to his designation for the ministry, but at the age of sixteen, showing signs of 'a weakly consumptive habit', the long-cherished plan had to be set aside and a different occupation found him. So he abandoned the study of the dead languages for the living, and learnt 'French, Italian, and High Dutch, without a master; and in the first and last of them I translated, and wrote letters, for an uncle of mine who was a merchant, and who intended to put me into a counting house in Lisbon. A house was actually engaged to receive me there, and everything was nearly ready for my undertaking the voyage. But getting better health my former destination for the ministry was resumed, and I was sent to Daventry, to study under Mr. Ashworth.' Besides the subjects mentioned above he learnt from another dissenting minister 'Geometry, Algebra, and various branches of Mathematics, theoretical and practical'. 'And at the same time I read, but with little assistance from him, Gravesande's *Elements of Natural Philosophy*, Watts's *Logic*,

[1] Priestley's *Hartley*, p. xlv.

Locke's *Essay on the Human Understanding*.' Meantime
he taught Hebrew to a neighbouring Baptist minister,
and also learnt Chaldee, Syriac, and began to read Arabic.
It is scarcely surprising that when admitted to the
Academy he was excused all the studies of the first year
and a great part of those of the second.

The welcome extended by Mrs. Keighley to all Dissenters had given Priestley many an opportunity of
listening to theological discussions. His own reading had
been wide, and at the age of eighteen he found himself no
longer a Calvinist but an Arminian. Liberal thought was
at work in the Anglican Church and among Nonconformist bodies. At the Salters Hall Synod in 1719 the
dissenting ministers in London, summoned to quell the
Arian controversy at Exeter, refused, by a majority, to
sign any confession of faith, thus leaving the door open
to progressive thought. Probably too many of them
were already infected with Arianism to wish to subscribe
to belief in the Trinity. Priestley had not advanced so
far as this, for as yet he still believed in the doctrines of
the Trinity, and of the Atonement. Mr. Haggerstone,
who had taught him mathematics, being a Baxterian, and
therefore believing that though some were elect for
salvation, others might attain it by their actions, was more
advanced than members of Priestley's own congregation,
and his general conversation was of a liberal turn, tending
to undermine his pupil's prejudices. Before leaving home
Priestley wished to be admitted a communicant of that
congregation in which he had been brought up, but his
heresy was already suspected. 'The elders of the Church',
he wrote, 'who had the government of it, refused me,
because, when they interrogated me on the *sin of Adam*,
I appeared not to be quite orthodox, not thinking that all
the human race (supposing them not to have any sin of

their own) were liable to the wrath of God, and the pains of hell for ever, on account of that sin only; for such was the question that was put to me.' The divergence of Priestley's views from those of his family made difficult the choice of an academy where he should be trained for the ministry. They wished him to go to that at Mile-end, but he opposed it as he would have to give an experience, and assent to ten articles of the strictest Calvinist faith, and re-sign his assent every six months. Fortunately Mr. Kirkby, the minister at Heckmondwycke, had little opinion of the scholarship of orthodox Dissenters and persuaded Mrs. Keighley to send her nephew to the academy kept by Dr. Doddridge at Northampton. But at this moment Dr. Doddridge died, and Priestley was entered for the academy under his successor, Dr. Ashworth, where he went in September 1752.

A recent writer[1] has said that when the complete history of education in England appears, no chapter will cause so much surprise as the one dealing with the period 1660–1800, which saw the rise of the dissenting academies. Legislation of the Restoration period closed the universities to Dissenters and at the same time tried to close the teaching profession to all save members of the Church of England. But Acts of Parliament were no more successful in preventing the ejected ministers from teaching than they were in silencing them. The need was great if the next generation of ministers was to receive a liberal education. So there gathered round many of the ministers those young men who wished to be their successors, and when the local magistrates decided to take action against them the minister went into hiding, or, if necessary, changed the site of his labours. Thus Richard Frankland

[1] Parker.

moved the site of his academy, founded at Rathmell in 1669, five times before the Toleration Act enabled him to return to Rathmell. The era of toleration, bringing comparative peace to the Dissenters, did not open to them the doors of the universities. Were dissenting parents to send their sons to Oxford and Cambridge they would have to consent to temporary conformity at least, and both the expense and the lack of discipline alarmed them. Thus the necessity arose of the academies undertaking the higher education of young men intended for other professions than that of the Dissenting Ministry, and training them for the Bar, medicine, and commerce.

Of dissenting academies none was more famous than that founded by Philip Doddridge at Northampton in 1729. It thrived from the very beginning, and in 1733 an attempt was made to close it on the grounds of the illegality of teaching in a grammar school without a bishop's licence. Doddridge refused to apply for the licence and appealed against the citation, but the persecution was stopped by the personal intervention of George II, who declared that 'in his reign there should be no persecution for conscience' sake'.[1]

Though an orthodox Trinitarian himself, Doddridge did not require the students to sign articles of faith as rigid [2] as those imposed in the universities, and admission was without tests. His assistant, Samuel Clark, held many heretical opinions, but Doddridge left him in charge both of the academy and congregation when ill-health necessitated his leaving Northampton,[3] and, on his death in 1752, and the subsequent removal of the academy to Daventry, Clark became assistant to Dr. Ashworth, Doddridge's orthodox successor.

[1] Parker.
[2] The articles would be the same as those required by the Toleration Act for a licence as nonconformist minister.   [3] Turner, *Lives of Eminent Unitarians*.

Daventry, lying on the northern borders of the open country of Northampton, was a Roman camp on the Watling Street, which in the eighteenth century was still one of the great highways of the kingdom, running from London to Chester and Holyhead. 'It is consequently', wrote Defoe, 'a great thoroughfare, and well furnished with good inns: for it subsists chiefly by the great Concourse of Travellers that pass that way.'[1] From Daventry on St. Bartholomew's Day, 1662, was ejected the Reverend Timothy Dod, 'a celebrated preacher, but in the latter part of his time was so very corpulent that he could not get up to the pulpit'. He was noteworthy for his piety and prayed seven times a day, 'twice with his whole family, twice privately with his wife, and three times alone'.[2] The present Independent Chapel was built in 1722, but dissenting meetings were held before this. Part of the buildings used for the academy was of older date and contained the necessary hiding place for an ejected minister. Here it was that Priestley spent the period of 1752 to 1755 'with that peculiar satisfaction with which young persons of generous minds usually go through a course of liberal study, in the society of others engaged in the same pursuits, and free from the cares and anxieties which seldom fail to lay hold on them when they come out into the world.'

The curriculum and discipline at Daventry was, no doubt, much the same as that at Northampton. Doddridge had begun the custom, which eventually came into general use, of giving all lectures in English instead of in Latin. During their first years at the academy the students followed a general course of study, but in the last they specialized for the Ministry, the Bar, medicine, or commerce. Natural and experimental philosophy was taught, as well as the more usual subjects of mathematics,

---

[1] Defoe, *Tour*, 3rd ed., ii. 361.   [2] *Calamy*, ii. 219.

history, and divinity. Languages were neglected, a fault which Priestley remedied by getting up early each morning to read Greek with a fellow student.

Students were expected to rise at 6 a.m. At 6.10 came roll-call and prayers followed by private reading till 8, when there was 'Family Prayer' and then breakfast. Lectures were given between 10 and 2. The afternoon, no doubt, was given to recreation. At 7 came evening prayer, followed by tutorials until 9, when supper took place. At 10 the gate was locked, and by 10.30 the students had to be in their rooms.

For failure to attend family prayer a student was fined 2*d*. Another fine was levied on students late for lecture, while he who cut a lecture was 'publicly reproved at the next meeting of the whole Society'. The authorities must have experienced rowdy students, for one regulation provided for the breaking of windows and 'furniture wantonly demolished'. The student who spread abroad reports 'to the dishonour of the family or any member of it' 'must expect a public reproof and hear a caution given to others to beware of placing any confidence in him'.[1] Fining was the usual method of punishment, but other methods might be resorted to 'for the intent of these laws is not to enrich the box at the expense of those who are determined to continue irregular, but to prevent any from being so'.

At Doddridge's Academy, and probably also at Daventry, the fees were £16 per annum for board and £4 for tuition. When pupils entered the academy 'they pay a guinea each for a closet and bring a pair of sheets. They find their own candles and put out their washing'. The student who drank tea in the morning must provide 'his own tea and sugar in just proportion as the company

[1] Parker, Appendix III.

shall agree', while the habit of making toast and butter and toasting cheese was found to be too expensive for students taken on ordinary terms.[1]

In Priestley's time both Dr. Ashworth and Mr. Clark were young as tutors went, and several of the students excelled them in certain branches of study. Priestley himself must have been a formidable pupil. So often the lectures had 'the air of friendly conversations on the subjects to which they related'. He found the intellectual life very stimulating.

'In my time, the academy was in a state peculiarly favourable to the serious pursuit of truth, as the students were about equally divided upon every question of much importance, such as Liberty and Necessity, the Sleep of the soul, and all articles of theological orthodoxy and heresy; in consequence of which all these topics were the subject of continued discussion. Our tutors were also of different opinions; Dr. Ashworth taking the orthodox side of every question, and Mr. Clark, the sub-tutor, that of heresy, though always with the greatest modesty.'

Priestley likewise 'saw reason to embrace what is generally called the heterodox side of almost every question', and before he left Daventry he had become an Arian, the extreme of heresy there, and his belief in the doctrine of the Atonement was more or less qualified.

Here Priestley first accepted the doctrine of necessity. He had learnt it originally from Anthony Collins, but was strengthened in it by Hartley's *Observations on Man*. Hartley's [2] belief that all things, both good and bad, were necessitated by the will of God, and were links in the great chain of cause and effect, which should culminate

---

[1] Ibid.   [2] Hartley will be dealt with more fully in a later chapter.

in some great and glorious end, was fully adopted by Priestley, and gave him that serenity of mind which never deserted him, however dark and unpromising might be his circumstances.

During his time at Daventry, Priestley made a number of lasting friendships. Chief of these was with 'Mr. Alexander of Birmingham', the student with whom he rose early to study languages, and who subsequently became one of the best Greek scholars of the age.[1] Unfortunately, Priestley left no record of how they spent their recreation except that they would speculate on the time when they would be dispersed through the country. During these years he never forgot that the chief object of his study was to fit himself for the duties of a Christian minister. He composed his first copy of his *Institutes of Natural and Revealed Religion* with the approval and assistance of Mr. Clark. His chance of success in the Ministry was lessened by the impediment in his speech which he inherited from his family, and which sometimes caused him to stammer.

'However, like St. Paul's *thorn in the flesh*, I hope it has not been without its use. Without some such check as this, I might have been disputatious in company, or might have been seduced by the love of popular applause as a preacher: whereas my conversation and my delivery in the pulpit having nothing in them that was generally striking, I hope I have been attentive to qualifications of a superior kind.'

[1] *D.N.B.*, John Alexander.

CHAPTER II

NEEDHAM MARKET AND NANTWICH

1755–61

NEEDHAM MARKET can have changed little since Priestley undertook his duties of dissenting minister there. Its long street of red-brick houses, lying in the pleasant Suffolk country beloved of Constable, a few miles to the north of Ipswich, probably possesses to-day an aspect very similar to that it had in the middle of the eighteenth century. But the old chapel has gone, and on its site stands a modern Congregational church. When Rutt visited it a hundred years ago personal recollections of Priestley had already disappeared.

It was a long journey to Suffolk from his Yorkshire home, but nevertheless it was with a light heart that Priestley set out for his first ministry. We can imagine with what longing and expectation the young man, dedicated to the Ministry from his childhood, embarked on his first charge. True he knew his congregation to be small, in the care of a superannuated minister, and the salary inconsiderable. His predecessor had received £40 a year, partly from the congregation and partly from the Presbyterian and Independent Funds. But the young Priestley felt that it would scarcely become him, whose views were heretical, to accept any grant from the orthodox Independent Fund. His congregation acquiesced and undertook to make good the deficiency, but, as he tells us, 'they deceived themselves; for the most part that I ever received from them was in the proportion of about thirty pounds per annum, when the expense of my board exceeded twenty pounds'. This refusal of the grant from the Independent Fund scarcely corroborated Timothy Priestley's statement that his brother had declared he had done his best while at Needham to hide his cloven hoof. But the congregation turned out to be less liberal than had been expected from their willingness to give up the grant.

Priestley settled down to his first winter's work with zeal, and for six months all went well. Besides the usual services he taught the children from Dr. Watts's Catechism. He opened a course of lectures on the theory of religion, from the *Institutes of Natural and Revealed Religion* written at Daventry. Here it was that he first failed in pleasing his congregation, for 'when I came to treat of the *Unity of God*, merely as an article of religion, several of my audience were attentive to nothing but the soundness of my faith in the doctrine of the Trinity'. His Arianism was easily discovered, for though he had avoided all subjects of controversy in the pulpit, he had never, in conversation, hidden his real opinions. The congregation decreased, and the old minister took its part against his successor. Happily the principal families remained true to him. His stammer also was a hindrance, and the neighbouring ministers would not exchange pulpits as the more genteel parts of their congregations objected to his ugly delivery, and absented themselves when he was to preach. 'But visiting that country some years afterwards, when I had raised myself to some degree of notice in the world, and being invited to preach in that very pulpit, the same people crowded to hear me, though my elocution was not much improved, and they professed to admire one of the same discourses they had formerly despised.'

Nevertheless Priestley was not altogether unhappy. He believed, then as always, that a divine providence was guiding his steps, 'that to them that love God all things work together for good'. He was happy in the family in which he lived, and he succeeded, as he always did, in making friends in the neighbourhood, not only with his own Nonconformist brethren but with others, including Mr. Chauvet, the rector of Stow-market, and Mr. S. Alexander, a Quaker. 'Here it was that I was first acquainted with any person of that persuasion; and I must acknowledge my obligation to many of them in every future stage of my life. I have met with the noblest instances of liberality of sentiment and the truest generosity among them.' Mr. Alexander was the owner of a good library to which Priestley had access, so he could devote himself to his studies, classical, mathematical, theological. He gave particular attention to the doctrine of the atonement, which, on leaving Daventry, he had believed only in a qualified sense. When he had finished his study he was of the opinion that it was supported neither by scripture nor by reason. He turned his observations into a treatise which a friend sent to Dr. Fleming and to Dr. Lardner. Part of Priestley's work they published under the title of *The Doctrine of Remission*, which was later embodied in an essay in the *Theological Repository*. Years afterwards, Priestley relates that when visiting Dr. Lardner, then a very old man, he asked him his opinion on this subject. Lardner took down a bundle of pamphlets and handed one to Priestley, saying that it contained his sentiment. It was Priestley's own.

The part Lardner had not approved of, and had not published, dealt with the reasoning of St. Paul. Priestley, becoming critical of the Apostle's reasoning, and wishing to regain faith in him, read Dr. Taylor's paraphrase on the Epistle to the Romans, but found no satisfaction in it. He published his remarks afterwards in the *Theological Repository*. Priestley argued that since the errors in the conduct of the best men in scripture are frequent and notorious there is no reason why their inspiration should exempt them from blame 'more in their writings than in their conduct'. Inspiration of their reasoning faculties would not answer its one valuable purpose of preventing men from falling into error, unless all translators and transcribers were also inspired. Priestley took many examples to illustrate the inconclusiveness of Paul's reasoning. For instance, he says that, while admiring the modesty and discretion of women who keep the place in the church where Paul had put them, he still appeals to their judgement, 'whether it be a sufficient reason for his peremptorily confining them to the place of hearers and learners, that *Adam* was first formed, and that Eve first transgressed.'[1]

Priestley's stammer did him one good service, as it was the cause of his first visit to London. Having seen the advertisement of a Mr. Angier, undertaking to cure all defects of speech, he prevailed on his aunt to pay the fee of twenty guineas. This was the last pecuniary assistance he ever received from her. Unhappily the cure was but temporary, and Priestley's speech lapsed into worse perplexities. During his London visit he made the acquaintance of Dr. Kippis and Dr. Benson, both of whom were of assistance in procuring for him the grant from various charities of an occasional £5, and both of whom he recollected as being true friends at a time when he stood most in need of them.

His first visit to London was scarcely likely to reconcile Priestley to Needham. He had met men of liberal thought who were occupied in intellectual work, and to return to the lack of sympathy which characterized his congregation must have been far from pleasant. He also felt deeply the pinch of poverty, for it was all that he could do to

[1] *Works*, vii. 407.

keep out of debt. So, in spite of the objections he had to the profession of schoolmaster, he decided to try it. He printed and distributed 'Proposals', but without any effect, 'not that I was thought to be unqualified for this employment, but because I was not orthodox'. So, being forced to renounce this scheme, he proposed giving lectures to grown persons in those branches of science for which he could procure the necessary means. He began with a course of a dozen lectures on the use of the globes at half a guinea, and just made enough to repay himself the cost of the globes. He intended continuing his lectures, and, as he could afford it, adding to his apparatus. But a change was nearer than he expected. Mr. Gill, a distant relation of his mother's, who had always been interested in him, and who knew his distressed condition, procured him an invitation to preach as candidate at Sheffield. Though no objection was made to his opinions there were some whose fastidious ears were displeased with certain real or supposed imperfections of delivery. They are also said to have objected to his 'gay and airy disposition', an accusation which is strengthened by his subsequent habit of jumping over the counter in the grocer's shop where he lodged at Nantwich.[1] The minister of the other Sheffield chapel, realizing that Priestley had no chance, told him he could procure him a year's invitation to preach at Nantwich in Cheshire. So in 1758 Priestley left Needham, and to save expense, went from Ipswich to London by sea.

Thus ended his first ministry. The young minister, who had set out so full of hope three years earlier, was now glad to shake the dust of Needham for ever from his feet, and with renewed faith in divine guidance, he set out to take charge of the even smaller congregation at Nantwich.

[1] Alexander Gordon, *Cheshire Classis Minutes,* p. 178.

Here Priestley found 'a good natured friendly people' with whom he spent three happy years. The black-and-white buildings of the old Cheshire town must have been a change from Suffolk. The chapel, built in 1726, still exists, and is the only building remaining in use among the Dissenters of all the chapels where Priestley ministered. It stands a little way back from the street and is built of red brick. Its interior is in the old meeting-house style, with pews and a fine pulpit of black oak. A tablet on the wall commemorates Priestley's ministry. He now opened a school where he had the instruction of thirty boys, and, at the same time, in a separate room, he taught 'half a dozen young ladies'. School-hours were from seven in the morning to four in the afternoon, and he never gave a holiday on any pretext whatsoever, 'the red letter days, as they are called, excepted'. Having become a schoolmaster, he took the greatest pains to excel at his profession, and found little time for any studies not connected with it. Out of school hours he took private pupils. He wrote an English grammar, leaving out all technical terms borrowed from foreign languages. But the best method of making his pupils proficient in the use of their own language, he told his friend, Caleb Rotheram, when seeking his advice on opening a school, was for them to write it, 'making the scholars compose dialogues, themes, &c., correcting their bad English, and making occasional remarks, I always found of most real use. Let them write fair copies of the English of many of their lessons, and omit no opportunity of making them write in their own language. This you will find pleasant to yourself, and of prodigious service to your pupils.' [1] He advised making a collection of books such as *Robinson Crusoe* which could be read out of hours. Though Priestley was scarcely rich

[1] Rutt, i. 64.

the success of his school made him affluent in comparison
with his circumstances at Needham. He was now able to
buy some scientific instruments, 'a small air pump, an
electric machine, &c.' He taught his scholars to keep
them in order and how to use them, and entertained the
parents with experiments, when his pupils were generally
the operators and often the lecturers. Thus he extended
the reputation of the school, though originally meaning
only to gratify his scientific leanings.

Besides the school there was the congregation to be
cared for. There were few children, not enough to make
worth while the organization of proper classes, and
Priestley contented himself with giving instruction in the
home. The congregation numbered about sixty, of
which some were travelling Scotsmen, whose company
was very pleasant to the young minister, and whom he
was surprised to find not at all Calvinistic. He boarded
with a Mr. Eddowes, whom, he says, was 'a very sociable
and sensible man, and at the same time the person of the
greatest property in the congregation, and who was very
fond of music'. Priestley was induced to learn the flute,
and, though he never became very skilful at it, he received
much amusement and pleasure from it through many
years of his life. He very charmingly remarked that he
would 'recommend the knowledge and practice of music
to all studious persons; and it will be better for them, if,
like myself, they should have no very fine ear or exquisite taste, as by this means they will be more easily
pleased, and be less apt to be offended when the per-
formances they hear are but indifferent'.

One drawback Nantwich shared with Needham, a lack
of intellectual and congenial society. Travelling in those
days was difficult, and, unless friends lived in the immediate vicinity, they were not likely to see much of each

other. Priestley had hardly a literary acquaintance beyond Mr. Brereton, a neighbouring clergyman. The dissenting ministers he most frequently met were Mr. Keay of Whitchurch and Dr. Harwood of Congleton, who was also a schoolmaster. With him Priestley made an exchange every six weeks during the summer months for the pleasure of spending one evening together. He also became acquainted with William Willetts, the dissenting minister of Newcastle-under-Lyme, who encouraged him in his scientific pursuits. Willetts had married a sister of Josiah Wedgwood, and the young potter was a frequent visitor at his house. Wedgwood's first meeting with Priestley may have occurred during one of these visits, but there is no record when and where they first became acquainted, only that by 1767 they were friends.

Another neighbour was Isaac Wilkinson of Wrexham. He had originally been a small farmer and overworker in an iron furnace at Clifton in Cumberland. In 1738 he had patented a laundress's box-iron, and, with the help of his son John, whom he had educated at Caleb Rotheram's [1] Academy at Kendal, laid the foundation of the family fortune by its manufacture. Isaac used to tell this story of his rise to prosperity.

'I worked at a forge in the North. My masters gave me 12*s*. a week: I was content. They raised me to 14*s*. I did not ask them for it. They went on to 16*s*., 18*s*.: I never asked them for the advances. They gave me a guinea a week! Said I to myself, if I am worth a guinea a week to you, I am worth more to myself! I left them, and began business on my own account—at first in a small way. I prospered. I grew tired of my leathern

---

[1] Father of Priestley's friend and correspondent.

bellows, and determined to make iron ones. Everybody laughed at me. I did it, and applied the steam engine to blow them; and they all cried out, "Who could have thought it".' [1]

Isaac had migrated to Wrexham, whence his younger son William attended the Nantwich school. But soon it must have been clear that it was neither solicitude for his pupil, nor respect for the father, but the attractions of Isaac's daughter Mary that caused the young schoolmaster's visits.

Thus passed three years, and with them Priestley's apprenticeship in the Ministry. His talents appeared more suitable for the academic than the pastoral office. As early as 1757 his knowledge of languages caused him to be recommended as tutor to the Warrington Academy, but he had been passed over in favour of Dr. Aikin, an older and more experienced man. In 1761 the trustees had once more to appoint a tutor in languages as Dr. Aikin had succeeded Dr. John Taylor as Divinity Tutor and principal. On whom could a better choice be made than on the young minister of Nantwich, of whose learning they had heard so much, and whose skill as a teacher was demonstrated in his flourishing school?

[1] Smiles, pp. 212–13 note.

CHAPTER III

WARRINGTON ACADEMY

1761–67

For some time Dissenters in the north of England had been alarmed at the state of their academies. So often private concerns, the death or retirement of the principal meant the end of the academy. Thus, when Dr. Caleb Rotheram died in 1751, and Dr. Latham in 1754, the academies at Kendal and Findern were closed, and Dissenters found themselves without any institution for higher education. To remedy this, the Rev. John Seddon, minister at Warrington, tried to interest the rich commercial and mercantile Dissenters of the northern towns in an academy which should be administered by trustees responsible to the subscribers, and which should provide a general education, as well as training for the Ministry, law, or medicine, and where complete absence of doctrinal tests should insure that condition of freedom necessary in any search after truth.

So new a venture was uncertain, and difficulties were increased by the traditional rivalry of Manchester and Liverpool, each fearing that the Academy might come too much within the other's sphere of influence. Liverpool wanted it at Ormskirk, and when Warrington was preferred, its citizens sulked and subscribed but half as much as did those of Manchester. But initial troubles were overcome, and the new academy was opened in the autumn of 1757, having for its first divinity tutor, with which office went the position of principal, Dr. John Taylor of Norwich. For twenty-four years he had ministered to that prosperous congregation at Norwich, which had recently built a new place of worship, the Octagon Chapel, at a cost of £5,000. Dr. Taylor's scholarship was extensive. His work on the Epistle to the Romans was an acknowledged authority. His great Hebrew concordance numbered among its subscribers the two English Archbishops and all except four of the bishops. Taylor was a spokesman of the liberal spirit characteristic of the rational Dissenters. He called on them to reject all names of sects and to call themselves '*Christians, and only Christians*',[1] and to pay attention rather to the things which unite than to those which divide. The claim to infallibility he denounced and derided whether found in 'Romish', 'Protestant', or 'Dissenting Popery'. The Dissenters should stand firm in liberty and love, with Christ alone as their leader, refusing all party schemes. They should 'establish their Faith, Practice, and Worship upon the Word of God alone as it shall from time to time be made known unto them'. 'But if ever they abandon Liberty and Love; if they stiffly adhere to Party-Names and Schemes; if they set bounds to Scripture-Knowledge, and presumptuously say, *Hither shalt thou go, and no further*: if they discourage the Honest and the Learned, that would throw in more Light and Truth among them, they will become weak, and waste and dwindle into nothing.'[2] He prefaced his divinity lectures with a charge to his students to think and judge for themselves, which is so illustrative of the purpose not only of Dr. Taylor, but of the promoters of the Academy, that it is well worth perusal.

'I do solemnly charge you, in the name of the God of Truth, and of our Lord Jesus Christ, who is the Way, the Truth and the Life, and before whose judgement seat you must in no long time appear, that in all

[1] Sermon preached at the opening of the New Chapel in Norwich, May 12th, 1756.
[2] *Defence of the Common Rights of Christians*, pp. 19 and 20.

your studies and inquiries of a religious nature, present
or future, you do constantly, carefully, impartially
and conscientiously attend to evidence, as it lies in the
Holy Scriptures, or in the nature of things and the
dictates of reason; cautiously guarding against the
sallies of imagination, and the fallacy of ill-grounded
conjecture. That you admit, embrace or assent to no
principle or sentiment, by me taught or advanced, but
only so far as it shall appear to you to be supported and
justified by proper evidence from Revelation, or the
reason of things. That if at any time hereafter, any
principle or sentiment by me taught or advanced, or by
you admitted and embraced, shall, upon impartial and
faithful examination, appear by you to be dubious and
false, you either suspect or totally reject such principle
or sentiment. That you keep your mind always open
to evidence; that you labour to banish from your
breast all prejudice, prepossession and party zeal; that
you study to live in peace and love with all your fellow-
Christians; and that you steadily assert for yourself,
and freely allow to others, the unalienable rights of
judgement and conscience.' [1]

But it is related that the good doctor, who had spent so
many arduous years in unravelling the scripture scheme,
could not believe possible disagreement with his conclusions. Perhaps Dr. Taylor was too old to begin work as a
teacher, but it is sad that the last years of so great a scholar
were embittered in the new position for which he had
resigned so much. Petty squabbles with the trustees
clouded the opening years of the Academy, and on Dr.
Taylor's death in 1761 a legacy of ill will was left behind,
which ultimately injured the Academy, for, as Priestley

[1] Quoted in *The Principles and Pursuits of an English Presbyterian Minister*,
p. 34.

remarked, 'all his friends, who were numerous, were our enemies.'

The original tutor in languages who succeeded to Dr. Taylor's position was Dr. John Aikin. His father, a native of Kirkcudbright, had settled in London as a draper, and intended his son for the same profession. But when the young man preferred the call of the Ministry, he was sent to Doddridge's Academy at Northampton, whence he proceeded to Aberdeen University. Later he was sub-tutor under Doddridge. A fall from his horse, causing injury to his chest, necessitated his abandoning the regular practice of the Ministry, and to his taking up that of a schoolmaster, and it was from his school at Kibworth that he came to Warrington.

Of the third tutor, Mr. Holt, who taught mathematics, very little is known. 'He is said to have been a man of remarkably mild and gentle manners, and of an equanimity almost unparalleled; in so much that he appears to have been scarcely capable of emotions, at least of any violent kind; to have been in short, a sort of reasoning automaton'.[1]

Priestley had been considered by the trustees as a possible lecturer in languages in 1757 when Dr. Aikin was preferred. His appointment in 1760 was eminently a wise choice, as Priestley was already well known for his learning. From his point of view it must have seemed but another witness of the divine goodness which he had not failed to trace even in unhappiness and loneliness. For the first time since his academic days he found himself in sympathetic surroundings. His colleagues held the same opinions and shared the same ideals with him. If disagreement arose on any point, they looked on controversy as a means of discovering the truth, and not as a sign of moral reprobation.

[1] *Monthly Repository*, 1813.

In his second year at the Academy on June 23rd, 1762, Priestley married Mary Wilkinson. He described his marriage as 'a very suitable and happy connexion, my wife being a woman of an excellent understanding, much improved by reading, of great fortitude and strength of mind, and of a temper in the highest degree affectionate and generous; feeling strongly for others, and little for herself.' Her great-granddaughter, Madame Belloc, declared her letters to be brighter than those of the Doctor, and from what little information we can gather we picture her as a woman of indomitable courage, and common sense and much humour.

The tutors and their families formed a congenial society. Every Saturday they drank tea together when the 'conversation was equally instructive and pleasing'. Though the Academy existed to support no particular opinion or belief the tutors were all 'zealous necessarians', likewise Arians, the only subject on which there was much difference was the doctrine of the atonement, 'concerning which Dr. Aikin held some obscure notions'. But intercourse was not confined to theological debates. 'Both "bouts rimés" and "vers de société"', wrote Miss Lucy Aikin, 'were in fashion with the set. Once it was their custom to slip anonymous pieces into Mrs. Priestley's workbag. One "copy of verses", a very eloquent one, puzzled all guessers a long time; at length it was traced to Dr. Priestley's self.' [1]

Aikin's daughter, Anna Laetitia, later Mrs. Barbauld, was first inspired by Dr. Priestley to try her hand at poetry, and acted the part of the poet laureate to the Academy.

Priestley sometimes visited both Manchester and Liverpool. At the latter he was usually the guest of Bentley, at

[1] Bright, *Historical Sketch of Warrington Academy*.

a later date Wedgwood's partner. Bentley, Priestley declared, was an unbeliever, though he was one of the prime movers in founding the Octagon Chapel, where a reformed liturgy was used, largely in the unfulfilled hope of attracting dissatisfied Anglicans. Whatever may have been the quality of Bentley's unbelief, it provided plenty of discussion between the two friends; and Priestley would break his rule of early bed in hope of giving his friend some of his faith in the divine guidance of the world.

Both Aikin and Priestley desired to make education a living thing, and to fill their pupils with a love of knowledge and a wish to acquire it. Both looked on education first of all to equip their students for life, and, as Christian ministers, they believed life should be lived nobly, in preparation for the life to come. They were born teachers, and were ready to take infinite trouble to make themselves understood and clear the ground of difficulties. Aikin's method was to lecture from some text-book. Every now and then he would stop and ask if he had made himself quite clear. If he had not, and difficulties were raised, he gave an explanation in quite a different manner. Should any student differ from his opinions, Aikin in no way reduced his regard or the trouble he took. Priestley has happily left an account of his methods of lecturing and the principles which inspired him. In *An Essay on a Course of Liberal Education for Civil and Active Life*, first published in 1765, he has recorded those ideals and objects which he believed should inspire education, and the methods which should be used. At the beginning of the essay Priestley remarked on the inadequacy of the educational system which provided pupils designed for a civil and active life, with an education only suitable for those who should follow a learned profession. The object of all education should be to fit men for life, 'for it is certainly our wisdom to contrive, that the studies of youth should tend to fit them for the business of manhood.'[1] Knowledge which would help men to be of service to their country was acquired anywhere except in the universities. Existing evils stood in need of redress; 'and let a person be reckoned a projector, a visionary, or whatever anybody pleases, that man is a friend of his country who observes and endeavours to supply any defects in the methods of educating youth'.[2] There were two subjects which Priestley wished introduced into the ordinary curriculum. The first was Civil History. Students should be taught the history of their own countries and times. The second was the important objects of 'Civil Policy; such as the theory of laws, government, manufactures, commerce, naval force, &c., with whatever may be demonstrated from history to have contributed to the flourishing state of nations, to rendering a people happy and populous at home, and formidable abroad'.[3] Priestley was making this suggestion within forty years of the foundation of a regius professorship of history at Oxford of which the holder was bound to pay out of his salary two lecturers in modern languages, sixty years before the foundation of a chair of economics, and more than a hundred years before modern history became a separate 'school'. He saw that a greater interest would be added when the students discovered that their studies dealt with subjects which were of general interest and often topics of conversation.

What sort of education should have been acquired by the student before entrance to the Academy? Priestley declares that he does not consider knowledge of the learned languages absolutely necessary though desirable, 'especially such an insight into Latin as may enable a

[1] *Lectures on History*, p. 9.   [2] Ibid., p. 10.   [3] Ibid., p. 11.

person to read the easier classics, and supersede the use of a dictionary, with respect to those more difficult English words which are derived from the Latin'; but the student 'should understand French very well' and have some knowledge of the 'more useful of practical mathematics'.[1]

The method of teaching which Priestley advocated was that practised by himself. The number of students in any class should not exceed twenty or thirty. An hour was long enough for any lecture. The lecturer should 'have a pretty full text before him, digested with care, containing not only a method of discoursing upon the subjects, but also all the principal *arguments* he adduces and all the leading *facts* he makes use of to support his hypothesis'.[2] Students should be encouraged to ask questions and make objections. Half the time should be employed in hearing the students give a minute account of the previous lecture. On all important questions references to the principal writers should be given, and in controverted issues, authorities on both sides. Occasionally the tutor should choose as subjects for 'orations, theses, or dissertations' important questions rising from the lectures.[3]

Priestley's most important work at Warrington was in his lectures on History and General Policy. These lectures, though delivered at Warrington, were not published until 1788, when many alterations and additions were made. Their value lies less in the material and facts which they contain than in their evidence of Priestley's attempt to introduce his students to wider realms. Priestley was not, and did not claim to be, an original historian. His lectures were composed from the standard works of the day which have long since been superseded, but it is interesting to note his insistence that the study of history

[1] Ibid., p. 15.   [2] Ibid., p. 20.   [3] Ibid., p. 21.

will be helped not only by the study of records, but of popular ballads, fiction, and the like.

Priestley regarded history primarily as a useful study. Not only should it amuse the imagination but it should improve the understanding. The experiences gathered from the past failures and successes of mankind should be of value to-day in pointing out the way we must go. Human nature is too complex a subject for *a priori* conclusions, and 'everything we can depend upon must be derived from facts'.[1] The science of government, which is so important to those who have at heart the interests of mankind, must be built on the solid foundations of facts provided by history—'Observation and experience are the only safe guides'. But the chief use of history is 'that it tends to strengthen the sentiments of virtue'.[2] The general view of events shows better than any partial glimpse that in this world virtue is its own reward. The study of the lives of great men will inspire us with the desire to rise above the level of mankind, while knowledge of their weaknesses will fill us with a proper humility. But above all Priestley trusted to history 'to strengthen the sentiments of virtue, by the variety of views in which it exhibits the conduct of Divine Providence, and points out the hand of God in the affairs of men'.[3] An event in which the casual observer sees but the blind play of chance Priestley recognized as an illustration of the inscrutable ways of God to man, who, from some small and trivial cause, educes a large and beneficient effect. 'Who would have imagined,' wrote Priestley, 'that the desire which Henry VIII had to be divorced from his wife would have brought about the Reformation in England?'[4] Among the most important objects of history to which Priestley drew the attention

[1] *Lectures on History*, p. 34.   [2] Ibid., p. 36.   [3] Ibid., p. 44.   [4] Ibid., p. 45.

of his pupils was political theory. We get the traditional treatment of the three forms of government—monarchy, aristocracy, and democracy—and it is easy to see the author's preference for the last. He did not believe in universal suffrage as he feared that to give the vote to men of no education or property would put fresh power in the hands of the unscrupulous managers of elections. Every voter should be required to write the name of the man he wished to vote for himself, and consequently every man of any ambition at all would acquire the arts of reading and writing.[1]

The attention of the reader is next directed to the study of the laws. Here Priestley does not show himself imbued with the spirit which was leading Beccaria and Bentham, Howard and Romilly to agitate for a more humane penal code. He looked on punishment to deter rather than to reform. In a note to his edition Rutt regretted 'that such a Christian philosopher and philanthropist as Dr. Priestley had not more maturely considered this subject'.[2] We may charitably suppose that this part has remained unaltered since these Warrington days. Priestley considered that 'a wise and prudent legislature' would try to prevent as well as punish, and he saw, as has many a Nonconformist before and since, the dangers which lurk in lotteries and the alehouse.

'Every thing is worthy of the attention both of a philosophical and political reader of history,' wrote Priestley, 'which can contribute to make a people happy at home, formidable abroad, or increase their numbers.'[3] Not least important is the study of economics. Between the original delivery of the lectures and their publication in book form had appeared Sir James Steuart's *Principles*

[1] Ibid. 1826 edition, p. 329. Note taken from American edition.
[2] Ibid., p. 288.   [3] Ibid., p. 220.

of Political Economy, the last great exposition of the mercantile theory, and, in 1776, the *Wealth of Nations.* Priestley admitted that he had extended this part of the lectures in the light thrown on the subject by these two works. The mere fact that he could accept two such different authorities shows that Priestley was not, on this subject, a profound thinker. But it should be noted that although Adam Smith stopped short of complete *laissez-faire* by excepting the usury laws, Priestley favoured their abolition. Bentham's *Defence of Usury,* which is supposed to have overthrown these laws, appeared about the same time, and neither Bentham nor Priestley could have been indebted to each other.

To the religious reader the noblest object is 'the conduct of Divine Providence in the direction of human affairs'.[1] There is no more presumption in searching history for evidence of God's ways than in scientific investigation. A comparison of the past with the present shows how much the conditions of life have improved. The reader has only to consider the increase of personal security and of personal liberty in the modern state.[2] Religion itself was not a suitable object for state organization. Priestley looked for the gradual and easy progress of truth and the spread of rational religion. He underestimated the stability of the establishment and did not realize the strength of the Methodist and Evangelical movements.

Though Priestley did not publish the *Essay on Government* till 1768, the year after he had moved to Leeds, so much of it touches on the same subject, as do the lectures on History, that it can well be considered here. Any student of the seventeenth and eighteenth century will know how common was the production of

[1] *Lectures on History,* p. 422.   [2] Ibid., p. 425.

political treatises. The seventeenth-century efforts to remodel the constitution on some different plan gave way under the House of Hanover to appreciation of the Revolutionary settlement. For a time advanced political thinking was left to the philosophers of France, and it was not until the first outbreak of the French Revolution that desire for radical reform became common. The apostle of the Glorious Revolution was John Locke. To him the Whigs traced their doctrine of trusteeship. While admitting that society existed for the preservation of property he had declared that government should be 'directed to no other end but the peace, safety, and public good of the people'.[1] Nor is this idea of the good of the people absent from other writers. Priestley had read the works of Locke, and it is not surprising to find that he whole-heartedly adopted the idea, and he tells us that 'the good and happiness of the members, that is, the majority of the members of any state, is the great standard by which every thing relating to that state must finally be determined'.[2] This may sound a commonplace, but it caught the imagination of one of Priestley's readers. Jeremy Bentham, still in his twenties, published in the wonderful year of 1776 his first book, *Fragment of Government*, where he first enunciated his famous doctrine of 'the greatest happiness of the greatest number'. In a later edition he acknowledged that it was the perusal of Priestley's Essay that had given him the idea. It is more than probable that had he not read the Essay he would have found the principle elsewhere. Nor did he find in Priestley the idea which was more peculiar to the radical philosophy that the people should be judges of their own happiness. It is this admission, meaning in practice the adoption of universal suffrage, which turned

[1] *Civil Government*, ch. ix.   [2] *Works*, xxii. 13.

eighteenth-century Whiggism into nineteenth-century Liberalism.

Part of the work deals with a suggestion that had been put forward for compulsory education. In those days, when the universities were the property of a sect, Priestley feared, and probably rightly, that any large state-aided system of education would be in the interest of the establishment, and he feared the consequent infringement of the liberty of the dissenting parent. Much of the Essay deals with the question of religion. As yet Priestley had not come to object to all forms of establishment under all circumstances, though objecting to the Anglican. He ridicules Warburton's defence of the civil magistrate's control of the Church. 'The Church,' Warburton had said, 'wants protection from external violence.' Priestley adds that it has had to pay a high price for security.

At the end of the Essay Priestley pleaded against binding futurity to our own opinions. Among his own small group of churches this has become an accepted maxim, but otherwise it seems to have made little headway in the world of religions, and the greater Christian churches are still bound, despite the advance of knowledge, to the dogma and doctrine of a by-gone age. But the freedom we claim from the dead hand of the past must be willingly extended to the future.

'Had even *Locke, Clarke, Hoadley,* and others, who have gained immortal reputation by their freedom of thinking, but about half a century ago been appointed to draw up a creed, they would have inserted in it such articles of faith as myself, and hundreds more, should now think unscriptural and absurd; nay, articles which they would have thought of great importance we should think conveyed a reflection

upon the moral government of God, and were in-
jurious to virtue among men. And can we think
wisdom will die with us? No: our creeds, could we be
so inconsistent with ourselves as to draw up any,
would, I make no doubt, be rejected with equal
disdain by our posterity.' [1]

To his eternal honour, Priestley pleaded for a complete
toleration of Catholics as well as of Protestants, when, as
yet, the idea was common with neither Dissenters nor
Anglicans. For all, whether 'Christians, Papists, Protestants, Dissenters, Heretics, or even Deists', Priestley
claimed 'the same liberty of thinking, debating, and
publishing'. There was no need to confine our neighbour within the limits which satisfied us. 'The wider we
make the common circle of liberty, the more of its friends
will it receive, and the stronger will be the common
interest.' [2]

It fell to Priestley's province to lecture on grammar
and oratory. His lectures on grammar were printed for
the use of the students. He attempted to make the
subject intelligible and useful to those unacquainted with
either Latin or Greek. The lectures on oratory and
criticism were published at the time when he was librarian
to Lord Shelburne and appropriately dedicated to Lord
Fitzmaurice. His object in lecturing on oratory was to
give his pupils directions for right speaking, though he
fully realized that practice was of paramount importance,
and instituted at Warrington public exercises. In the part
that deals with criticism his references show him to have
been well acquainted with English literature and more
especially with Shakespeare and Milton, but he seems to
have been more interested in the mechanism than in the

---

[1] *Works*, xxii. 126.   [2] Ibid. xxii. 137.

inspiration of poetry. In spite of his early ignorance of fiction he had now read the standard works, but enjoyed fiction for its moral rather than its own sake. He criticized Richardson for his treatment of Lovelace in *Clarissa Harlowe*, and accused him of making his villain so attractive that we can forgive his ill-treatment of any other woman save Clarissa. The lectures were not profound, but they were an honest attempt to introduce young men to the glories of their own language.

It was at this time that Priestley began the regular habit of spending a month of each year in London. He was naturally enough received into that circle of rational dissent and liberal politics whose chief adornments were Richard Price and Benjamin Franklin. The latter is too well known a character to need describing here. His influence in starting Priestley along the new road of scientific discovery cannot be underestimated. Richard Price, an influential thinker and a man of wide fame, is scarcely remembered to-day outside the circle of the professional historian. Like Priestley, he had been brought up in Calvinist surroundings, but had rejected the orthodox view of the Trinity for the more liberal Arian. For long he had believed any pursuit which interfered with the direct service of God to be sinful, and consequently held his love of mathematics to be unholy. But the widespread havoc and misery caused by the failures of the bubble insurance companies led him to apply his mathematical training to the subject of insurance.[1] Most insurance companies were based on plans 'alike improper and insufficient', and the foundation of actuarial science was only fully laid by the publication of his work, *Observations on Reversionary Payments*, published in 1771. One of the results was that Price was

[1] Thomas, p. 53.

asked to reorganize the Equitable Society.[1] For many
years, his biographer tells us, he might be seen daily
riding from his home at Newington Green to the offices
of the society at Blackfriars Bridge on his favourite
white horse and wearing a blue greatcoat and black
spatter-dashes; the carmen and orange-women could be
heard saying, 'There goes Dr. Price, make way for Dr.
Price'.[1] Like so many of the Dissenters, his sympathies
were with the American colonies, and his pamphlet,
Civil Liberty, is said to have been one of the causes of the
Declaration of Independence, the policy which he
advocated. He was asked by the American government
to take charge of their finances, but declined, and the
University of Yale honoured him with the. degree of
LL.D. on a day when the only other recipient was George
Washington. Difficulty has been found in judging
whether Price was more remarkable for the qualities of
his head or of his heart. Suffice it to say that all who came
into contact with him were impressed by the beauty of his
character, and that to his contemporaries he was the
great and good Dr. Price.[2] It was natural that this liberal
theologian, likewise Fellow of the Royal Society, should
find much in common with Priestley. Though later
their religious differences widened, and Price opposed
Priestley's metaphysical scheme, they never lost either
affection or regard for each other, and gave a good
example of how controversy might be carried on.

Priestley had always had a hankering after natural
philosophy. The friendship with Price and Franklin
introduced him to scientific society, and it was with
Franklin's sympathy that he undertook to write the
history of electricity. From writing about the discoveries
of others he began to experiment for himself, originally

[1] Ibid. p. 57.   [2] Ibid. p. 149.

only with the purpose of settling controversial points. He was consulted by Wedgwood on the possibility of gilding by electricity. His history led to his own election to the Royal Society in 1766, an event which brought him into close contact with the leading scientific minds of the age. His friends helped him by providing the necessary books: Benjamin Vaughan remembered having helped to unpack in the Doctor's kitchen at Warrington a box of books worth £50, into which the bookseller had inserted the name of Sir George Savile as a hint as to the donor. At the time of writing the *History of Electricity* five hours a day were regularly employed in lecturing in public or private, and yet Priestley was able to supply Franklin with a copy of the *History* within a year of undertaking it. This is a pretty clear proof of the speed at which he worked, as well as of the time devoted to his labours.

A year earlier, in 1765, he had been made LL.D. by the University of Edinburgh in recognition of his 'Chart of Biography'.

Unfortunately, neither hard work nor progressive ideas led to the prosperity of the Academy. Priestley's salary was but £100 a year and a house and what he could make from taking boarders at £15 a year. The trustees did not find it easy to collect subscriptions, nor were the methods always very business-like, no statement of accounts being sent to the supporters.[1] In Priestley's day the breakdown of discipline, which later was so marked, had not yet taken place, and incidents like the following did not occur until a later period.

'One morning the landlords of the different inns in Warrington might have been seen with bewildered

---

[1] *Monthly Repository*, viii. 287.

looks gazing up to the signboards which swung above their hospitable doors. Well might they be bewildered! In a single night the "Red Lion" had become the "Roebuck", the "Nag's Head" was the "Golden Horseshoe", the "Royal Oak" had changed places with the "Griffin", and the "George and the Dragon" appeared now as the "Eagle and Child". Another story is told of a most respectable lady who was coming from a ball. Her carriage stops the way—she is stepping towards it. But—what and how is this? The footmen are devil's imps, with torches in their hands; the coachman grins down with a demon's face from the box; and from the carriage comes forth to escort the lady home a terrible figure, but one easy to be recognized, with horns and tail and cloven feet. One student procured a black ox skin, and haunted Bank Street night after night, till houses were deserted and Bank Street half ruined.' [1]

On May 18th, 1762, Priestley had been ordained as dissenting minister, and from time to time he preached in the neighbourhood. Sometimes in Seddon's absence he acted as his curate, taking the services and burying the dead, though keeping the perquisites for the regular minister. Now, finding the salary at Warrington insufficient to support a growing family and a delicate wife, he decided to resume the work of the Ministry, and accepted the invitation of the Mill Hill congregation, Leeds, whither he went in September 1767.

[1] Bright, *Historical Sketch of Warrington Academy.*

CHAPTER IV

LEEDS

1767–73

O N March 15th, 1672, Charles II issued his Declaration of Indulgence, suspending all penal laws against Nonconformists and Popish Recusants. Charles II claimed to set aside, by right of his royal prerogative, those laws known as the Clarendon Code, which had been passed by the Restoration Parliament under the leadership of the Earl of Clarendon. Some of the harassed and persecuted Dissenters hesitated whether they should accept toleration of such doubtful legality, especially as it extended to Popery. On the other hand many welcomed it, even should Atheists and Catholics enjoy it as well, agreeing with Oliver Heywood, 'we have liberty to do good, as they have to do hurt'.[1] For the most part the Dissenters were content to worship in private houses licensed for the purpose, for they were neither wealthy nor powerful enough to undertake the building of meeting-houses. But there were exceptions, and among these were the Presbyterians of Leeds, who built near the Alms-house garth a 'meeting house, commonly called the New Chapel . . . It is said to be the first, and it is certainly one of the stateliest Fabricks (supported by a Row of Pillars and Arches, More Ecclesiarum), built upon that occasion in the North of England'.[2] The first recorded service was held on March 25th, 1674. In subsequent, as in former, periods of persecution Leeds was never completely without its Ministry, and after the Toleration Act the chapel at Mill Hill flourished.

Like all the Presbyterian congregations Mill Hill began

---

[1] Quoted by Charles Wicksteed, *Lectures on the Memory of the Just*, p. 30.
[2] Ibid., p. 31, quoting Thoresby, *Ducatus Leodensis*.

by being orthodox in doctrine, but, during the ministry of the Rev. Thomas Walker (1748–63), it changed its position. Walker was an anti-trinitarian, and doubted 'the doctrine of the atonement and of the innate depravity of human nature'.[1] By his liberal doctrines he lost many members of his congregation, but he built up that 'liberal, friendly, and harmonious' congregation which so pleased his successor Priestley.[2]

The call to the Mill Hill congregation must have seemed almost like a summons home. Priestley had grown up within six miles of Leeds. An uncle had drilled the Mill Hill volunteers at the time of the Forty-Five, and he had translated letters for an uncle for whose counting house at Lisbon he was intended. The famous Cloth Market, 'which is indeed a Prodigy of its Kind, and is not to be equalled in all the World', to see which 'many Travellers and Gentlemen have come over from Hamburgh, nay even from Leipsick in Saxony',[3] would have been familiar to Priestley since the days of his childhood, and no doubt he drew a large part of his congregation from the merchants and manufacturers and artisans of the wool trade.

His return to the Ministry led Priestley once more to the study of theological questions. He carefully read Dr. Lardner's *Letter on the Logos* and 'became what is called a Socinian'. The purpose of the *Letter* was primarily to refute the Arian hypothesis of the pre-existence of Christ. Dr. Lardner did not deny the miraculous birth, and in fact adduces it along with miracles and the Resurrection as evidence of the divine mission. What Lardner wished to prove was that Christ had a human soul, and became Son of God, and was exalted above all others on account of, and as reward for, his sufferings upon earth.

[1] Schroeder, *Mill Hill Chapel.*   [2] *Memoirs.*   [3] Defoe, *Tour*, 1927 ed. ii. 611.

Priestley had always looked on the calling of a minister of the Gospel as the highest that could fall to the lot of man. He now threw himself, heart and soul, into his profession. The children and young people were divided into three classes of catechumens. For the use of his older pupils he rewrote the *Discourses on Natural and Revealed Religion*, and for the younger composed his own catechism.[1] Compared with the *Shorter Catechism*, its theology is simple. It aimed at inculcating upon young minds good moral habits rather than doctrine. Priestley never ceased regarding heaven and hell as the reward of, rather than as the result of, good or bad conduct. In his later years he came to believe that the end of all the human race would be happiness, yet in this catechism we find the small child learning 'If I have been wicked, I shall go to Hell, where I shall be very miserable'.

Priestley also attended to the spiritual welfare of the older members of his flock. He was grieved at their small attendance at the 'Lord's Supper'. Believing this to be due to the superstitious ideas connected with the Mass and Holy Communion among various sects, Priestley attempted to show the corruption that had arisen round the celebration of the Lord's Supper since Apostolic times. He held that the express command of Christ made its observance obligatory upon all Christians, but, nevertheless, it was neither more efficacious nor more sacred than other forms of prayer or worship. Once the idea of the magical efficacy of the bread and wine was done away with no more preparation was needed for it than for any other service. The Lord's Supper is 'a solemn but cheerful rite, in remembrance of Christ',[2] and should be attended by all 'professing Christians'.[3] The only opinion implied by attendance was 'that Christ is a

[1] *Works*, xxi.   [2] Ibid. xxi. 259.   [3] Ibid. xxi. 261.

teacher sent by God; that it is a profession of a man's being simply a Christian, and not of his attachment to any particular sect or denomination of Christians'.[1] Although Priestley wrote for his congregation alone, such a simplification of Christianity could not escape attack, and consequently he was drawn into controversial writings. The *Gentleman's Magazine* declared his Christian to differ from a Deist only in a speculative opinion[2]. He was attacked by the Rev. Henry Venn, Vicar of Huddersfield and grandfather of that Henry Venn who ministered to the 'Clapham Sect'. The Rev. Samuel Palmer of Hackney took up the challenge on behalf of the orthodox Dissenters, but there was nothing bitter in his reply, and Priestley treated him as an ally rather than as an enemy. Later Priestley held that in the Primitive Church children had been admitted to Communion, and he urged the Dissenters to return to this practice.

To one brought up in Calvinistic surroundings the loosening of Church discipline among the rational Dissenters was a cause for anxiety. We find Priestley writing to persuade his congregation to tighten the reins of discipline. He deplored the position into which the minister had sunk and declared that he was now 'considered as a person who is paid by his hearers for haranguing them once a week'.[3] Should any members of his congregation find his views displeasing it was open to him to go where he would be better satisfied. Priestley wanted a liberal education for his minister, and considered that he should be able to pray, preach, and expound the Scriptures. In the management of the congregation he should be assisted by ten or twenty elders. It should

[1] Ibid. xxi. 262.   [2] *Gentleman's Magazine*, 1768, pp. 338–40.
[3] *Works*, xxi. 405.

fall to the elder 'to admonish all members of the society that live within his district or neighbourhood, of every irregularity, or tendency to it, with prudence and discretion'. Only notorious offenders should be 'proposed to the whole society for public censure'.[1] Even when the society was forced to its last resource, excommunication, the offender should not be cut off from the benefit of public prayer. It does not seem to have occurred to Priestley that the offender who did not repent before a public censure would scarcely be likely to continue his connexion with a voluntary society. His scheme for Church discipline, had it been adopted, would have made rational Dissent as illiberal, if not as powerful as Scottish Presbyterianism. Happily Priestley was fighting against the spirit of the age, and his scheme was not accepted. He did not think very much would come of it, and expected 'to be very much laughed at' on account of it. 'However,' he wrote to Samuel Merivale, 'I seriously meant well in it, and hope it will do some good; if not in directing to the *means*, yet in setting the *end* in a light of greater importance.'[2]

Other aspects of the decline of Dissent caused Priestley to publish in 1769, at the instigation of Doctor Kippis and Doctor Price, *A Free Address to Protestant Dissenters*. 'Sorry I am, from a regard to the interests of truth and liberty, to see the zeal of many so cool in so noble a cause, for which our heroic ancestors sacrificed so much.'[3] The deserters, Priestley declared, were more numerous among those who differed much than among those who differed little from the doctrines of the Established Church. He looked to the Dissenters in all countries to advance the cause of truth; in establishments the power of the civil magistrate was always too strong for reformation and

---

[1] *Works*, xxi. 425.   [2] Rutt, i. 125.   [3] *Works*, xxii. 252.

'the remonstrances of a thousand *candid disquisitors*, followed by as many *confessionalists*, will signify but little'.[1] The Protestant Dissenters should regard their position with respect, for among them 'alone, in this country, is the worship of the only living and true God known and the purity of the Christian doctrine and discipline exhibited'.[2] The Dissenter, not bound by subscription to articles of faith, might alter his opinions without any formal recantation. Since his emoluments did not depend on assent to any creed, he had not to choose between the disagreeable alternatives of prevaricating with his conscience or of renouncing his livelihood. The rational Dissenter, being of a liberal turn of mind, condemned no man for his religious opinions, since he believes that all honest men stand well with their Maker. But it does not follow that because 'there is no harm to them in their worship, there is no harm to you in it'.[3] Occasional attendance at church is permissible: 'I have frequently gone to church myself, and do not scruple to go sometimes still, though I am shocked by what I hear there'.[4] But this was a different matter from habitually joining in the service.

Since the rational Dissenter is separated from the Conformist on important questions of faith, it is his duty to propagate his opinions 'and write with the simplicity and fearless integrity of a Christian, openly asserting the great doctrines of the proper unity of God, and equity of his moral government, in opposition to what is in reality Tritheism, and the doctrines of absolute predestination and reprobation, by whomsoever they may be held.'[5] It was impossible to show the truth of

[1] Ibid. xxii. 256. Priestley is referring to *Free and Candid Disquisitions relating to the Church of England* by Rev. John Jones of Alconbury, published 1749, and to *The Confessional* by Archdeacon Blackburne. [2] Ibid. xxi. 257.
[3] Ibid. xxii. 258. [4] Ibid. xxii. 259. [5] Ibid. xxii. 268.

one set of opinions without proving the falsity of the contrary. An age of indifference and infidelity had branded religious controversy as impolite, and he 'who loves his religion, and values the purity of it; and who expresses his generous indignation at the usurpations of some, and the servility of others with respect to it, must be called a *bigot* and an *illiberal-minded* person'.[1]

The laity should assist the cause with generosity. The ministers without adopting the austerity of their ancestors should live simply. They should place their profession before the pursuit of the polite arts or of science, and even speculative theology should be second to the advancement of virtue among their hearers.[2]

Priestley next turned to attack Blackstone who, in the famous *Commentaries*, had declared that the principles of the Protestant Dissenters made bad citizens. Blackstone did not usually reply to his critics, but in this case he made an exception. While vindicating his statement of the law he agreed that his strictures were open to a misunderstanding. The passage was intended to refer to earlier Dissenters, but it might seem to infer a general reflection on the 'Spirit, the Doctrines, and the Practice of our modern Dissenters'. In subsequent editions of the *Commentaries* the passage was modified. But though 'the Doctor, in his *Reply*, has openly disavowed the sentiments, and generously promised to cancel the offensive paragraphs', Priestley undertook for the benefit of his fellow citizens, who shared the Doctor's beliefs, an exposition of the principles of the Dissenters. This pamphlet, he held, was 'the freest and boldest thing I ever wrote'.[3] Because the Dissenter disclaimed all authority in matters of religion he does not, Priestley declared, deny human authority in civil matters. 'We Dissenters consider our

---

[1] *Works*, xxii. 269.   [2] Ibid. xxii. 285.   [3] Rutt, i. 103.

interest, the laws we are bound by, and the authority we submit to, with respect to the things of *this world* and those of *a future,* to be quite independent of one another.'[1] 'As Dissenters we have no peculiar principles of civil government at all.'[2] Since the time of the Revolution the sympathies of the Dissenters had been with the court, 'except in some of the last years of Queen Anne, and in the year 1733, when the Excise Bill was in agitation'.[2] At the present time many of the Dissenters, through their old loyalty to the House of Hanover, support the Ministry, 'and did so more especially before the late vote of the House of Commons in favour of Mr. Luttrel.'[3] This interference with the freedom of election, 'the very basis of our liberty,'[3] alarmed many, 'and at present the Dissenters, I believe, are about as much in opposition to the court, as the rest of the nation'.[4] Many of them and generally the whole body of Quakers refuse to oppose the court to avoid irritating it into starting a new persecution. On the whole they 'are well satisfied with their present situation' and 'are glad to purchase their religious liberty by their exclusion from civil offices'.[4]

No pamphleteer, provided he is read, can expect to escape unanswered. Priestley found an opponent in the Rev. William Enfield, then a minister at Liverpool, and later tutor at Warrington Academy. Enfield now published anonymously *Remarks on several late Publications relative to the Dissenters in a Letter to Dr. Priestley.* He considered Priestley fiery and over hasty, and feared the cause of peace between the Established Church and Nonconformity would be endangered by Priestley's polemics. The dissenting interest was not the only interest in favour of 'truth, liberty, and religion'. Where

[1] *Works,* xxii. 351. [2] Ibid. xxii. 354. [3] Ibid. xxii. 355.
[4] Ibid. xxii. 361.

E

Nonconformity was distinguished from the Establishment was in its claim to private judgement in matters of religion. Dissenting churches were often only nominally free, and further progress in religious matters was often impeded by 'bigoted attachment to the system of opinions, or modes of worship in which we have been educated.' The ministers also feared to displease their congregations and lose their salaries. Enfield was no more orthodox than was Priestley. He held that religious knowledge was capable of growth. 'All knowledge is progressive; every art and science is capable of improvement. Why then should it be imagined that we have reached our *ne plus ultra* in religion?'[1] Priestley did not allow these strictures to go unanswered, and in 1770 published his reply. He returned to the charge of idolatry which he had brought against the Anglican Church and which had so much offended Enfield. He thought that Enfield had justified conformity to the Church of England on such grounds as would justify conformity with the Church of Rome. Priestley declared that he considered '*subscription* to articles of faith which a man does not believe (by which I mean a subscription to them as the means of getting a livelihood, or raising a fortune)'[2] to be a vice of the most malignant nature. 'A man who can thus tell a deliberate lie, and really think it justifiable, must, on the same principle, be able to justify any actions of a similar nature' and thus he may 'deceive and impose upon mankind in the most essential respects'.[3] Priestley was amused at Enfield coming to the rescue of the Church of England while an Anglican (Mr. Venn) had defended the orthodox Nonconformists, and for the future he thought he might pair off his antagonists against each other.[4]

[1] Enfield.   [2] Works, xxii. 423.   [3] Ibid. xxii. 423.   [4] Ibid. xxii. 439.

Priestley realized the unpopularity of these writings.

'My piece', he wrote to Lindsey, 'will give more offence to a very considerable part of those who are called rational Dissenters than you can imagine. By one means or another, I believe I have more enemies among the Dissenters than in the Church. I shall soon be obliged to court the Papists and the Quakers in order to have any friends at all, except a few philosophical persons, who like his Grace,[1] know nothing of my having meddled with theology or politics.'[2]

Priestley's controversy with Enfield was not of a personal character. He was always capable of disputing bitterly and remaining friends with any one. The next year we find him writing 'Mr. Enfield and I are upon very good terms. I really esteem him much'.[3]

His gift for friendship was well exercised at Leeds, where Priestley found sympathetic friends in the neighbouring dissenting ministers. Both Turner of Wakefield and Newcome Cappe of York were collaborators with him in the *Theological Repository*, and Graham of Halifax was an old friend, being one of the most heretical ministers who had enjoyed Mrs. Keighley's hospitality. Early in the summer in 1769 Turner and Priestley went on a visit to Archdeacon Blackburne[4] at Richmond. The Archdeacon was a liberal-minded man and famous as the author of *The Confessional*. This book, first published anonymously in 1766, attacked the whole system of subscription to articles of faith. It gave the impetus, if it did not start, the demand from Parliament for relief from subscription to the Thirty-Nine Articles. It also spoilt all chance of further advancement for its author; Secker,

[1] Duke of Northumberland.   [2] Rutt, 118, 1770, Aug. 30.
[3] Ibid. i. 143.   [4] Francis Blackburne (1705–87).

Archbishop of Canterbury, publicly declaring so at his own table.[1]

It was on the occasion of this visit that Priestley first met Theophilus Lindsey and began a friendship that later he declared to have been 'the source of more real satisfaction to me than any other circumstance in my whole life'.[2] At this time Lindsey was vicar of Catterick, to which he had been collated in 1763. The fresh subscription that was demanded on this occasion renewed his doubts in regard to the articles of the Church. By the time that Priestley met him he was already persuaded that many things demanded by the Church of England were unscriptural. Still he shrank from leaving a church, which, in spite of imperfections, he loved. Lindsey was a man of humble nature. He knew that others whom he revered, holding similar opinions to his own, had not found it necessary to leave the Church. He was devoted to the service of his flock; he was an exemplary parish minister, and a pioneer of Sunday schools. His wife, a step-daughter of Archdeacon Blackburne, was a delicate woman, and it was but natural that he should hesitate before renouncing his means of livelihood. And in 1769 there was still hope of relief from Parliament.

Priestley's letters to Lindsey begin very soon after this first meeting. From this time he frequently sought Lindsey's advice and criticism before publishing, and as the years went by he came more and more to rely upon the judgement of his quieter and gentler friend. Not that there was any lack of character about Lindsey. He enjoyed argument as much as Priestley, and, unlike the Archdeacon, 'Friend Lindsey can talk and even dispute on horseback. In that situation I am sure to

---

[1] See Memoir prefixed to *Blackburne's Works*.
[2] Rutt, i. 82.

fall into reveries, and often forget both myself and company.'[1]

Soon after his settlement at Leeds the idea of a theological magazine occurred to Priestley. The scheme received support from the leading dissenting ministers, approved by Dr. Aikin and Dr. Price, and was undertaken with the concurrence of Cappe of York, Turner of Wakefield, Scott of Ipswich, author of several hymns still in use, Samuel Merivale, tutor of the dissenting College at Exeter, Samuel Clark of Birmingham, Priestley's old tutor, and Andrew Kippis of Westminster, one of the most important ministers of the metropolis and editor of the *Biographia Britannica*. In the preface to the first number Priestley pointed out the need of periodical publications in all branches of knowledge. In order to publish a few criticisms on a small part of the Bible it was necessary to write a whole book. The *Theological Repository* was 'meant to be a common channel of communication, which shall be open for the reception of all new observations that relate to theology'. Writers of every shade of opinion might contribute to its columns. It was open to the non-Christian as well as to the Christian. It would be printed occasionally and 'sold for six-pence, one shilling, or more, as the materials that are sent it shall make it necessary'.

The *Repository* drew its contributors largely from the ranks of the dissenting ministry. Most of those mentioned above wrote regularly. Another contributor was the Rev. Mr. Cardale of Evesham, who was apparently more renowned for his learning than for his success in the Ministry, and who had 'about twenty people to hear him at the last, having ruined a fine congregation by his very learned, critical, and dry discourses, an extreme heaviness

[1] Belsham, p. 22.

in the pulpit, and an almost total neglect of pastoral
visits and private inspection'.[1] We find Lindsey writing
under the signature of Patrobas, and, of course, the
editor was a profuse contributor. The paper on the Doctrine of the Atonement, which he had published when
minister at Needham, now made its reappearance, and the
attack on the Reasoning of St. Paul, written at the same
time, was also inserted in the *Repository*. These papers
drew forth replies, and the controversies must have pleased
Priestley, believing as he did that the outcome of such
arguments would be a victory for truth over error.
During its life Priestley contributed to the *Repository*
many papers under various signatures.

The demand for such a work was small. It probably
made little appeal beyond the borders of rational dissent.
The higher orders of the Anglican Church preferred,
when possible to overlook the publications of their
opponents. The Deists, who, Priestley hoped, would
voice their objections to Christianity, and give him the
opportunity of converting them, a result he believed
bound to follow his statement of the facts, ignored the
Repository. Behind Priestley was no trust nor rich individual to finance the scheme. We may surmise that he
received financial help at an early date, but still the main
loss incurred in the publication fell on him. In his first
extant letter to Lindsey, which Rutt dates 'soon after
Oct. 1769',[2] Priestley wrote 'I am much obliged to the
friends of this work for their generous offer of assistance.
There will be occasion for it: but if the work ever answer,
the money shall be returned.'[3] The next year he wrote
that he would be a loser, but expected help. He would
state the account to a few friends, 'but I am advised not

[1] *Orton Letters*, i. 154.   [2] Rutt, i. 102.
[3] Ibid. i. 118.

to make it public lest our enemies should triumph'.[1] By
the end of the year he was more hopeful of success and
wrote to Lindsey 'it shall not die, if there be a possibility
of keeping it alive'.[2] 'But in spite of various hopes,'[3] by
April, 1771, he was sure that he must bring the publication
to a close, for 'I do not find that there is any prospect of
the sale of this work increasing, and, therefore, that I
shall be obliged to shut it up, at least for some time'.[4]
With the publication of the third volume the first series
of the *Theological Repository* ended. Its demise was a
disappointment, and Priestley was determined to revive
it as soon as possible. As early as 1774 he wrote to Mr.
Cardale of Evesham: 'Dr. Kippis is about to review the
Repository and thinks it would gratify the public, and
facilitate the revival of the scheme, if he was authorized
to give the names of the principal writers.'[5] Ten years
were to elapse before he resumed its publication.

Priestley's last years at Leeds coincided with the effort
made by a number of Anglican clergy and professional
men to obtain relief from subscription to the Thirty-
Nine Articles. It was a movement within the Church, but,
as its leaders were Blackburne and Lindsey, and as its
failure gave fresh impetus to the rising cause of Unitarianism, it is not altogether without interest in the life of
Priestley.

The Church of England, no more than the dissenting
churches, had escaped the influence of the broadening
theological outlook which characterized the opening of
the eighteenth century. Arianism, in itself as dogmatic as
Trinitarianism, made headway within the established
church, and reached its zenith in Dr. Clarke. The lack of
formularies had made it easy for the Arian to 'creep and

[1] *Dr. Williams' Library MSS.*   [2] Rutt, i. 120.
[3] *Dr. Williams' Library MSS.*   [4] Ibid.   [5] *Belloc-Lowndes MSS.*

intrude, and climb into' the Dissenting fold. It should have been more difficult to scale the walls of the Establishment, protected as they were by the Thirty-Nine Articles set up by Act of Parliament. The intrusion was made at a cost of honesty, the price always paid by liberals or modernists who remain within the Church. The Articles, assent to which was necessary to obtain a livelihood and preferment, were signed, but he who signed accepted them in some different meaning either to that shown by the words or meant by the original authors. There must have been many simple souls to whom this casuistry was abhorrent.

In 1766 Archdeacon Blackburne had published *The Confessional*. In it he investigated the position of articles of faith in Protestant churches, and the Anglican articles in particular. He especially attacked the Arminians, Arians, and others who signed the articles intending a different meaning to that of their framers, and in another place declared that the casuistry arising from subscription would help 'posterity in forming a true judgement of the *liberal sentiments* of the present age on the article of *moral honesty*, as well as give them a just idea of our *improvements in theology*, and how far we go beyond the *zeal* and *dexterity* of our forefathers, in accommodating *plain, simple, naked* Christianity, with the arts, ornaments, opulence, power, and policy, of the kingdoms of this world'.[1] This book went quickly through several editions and gave rise to the demand that relief from subscription should be sought from Parliament.

Lindsey's uneasiness at his position had grown. Already when he first met Priestley he had made up his mind that resignation was the only course open to him. Strangely enough, Priestley, who had attacked the con-

---

[1] *The Confessional*, pp. 526-31.

forming but disbelieving clergy in print, did not attempt to persuade him to leave the church. On the contrary, when Lindsey first disclosed his intention he 'was not forward to encourage him in it, but rather advised him to make what alterations he thought proper in the offices of the church, and leave it to his superiors to dismiss him if they chose. But his better judgement, and great fortitude, led him to give up all connexion with the Established Church of his own accord.'[1] Lindsey postponed his resignation, as he did not wish to take such an irrevocable step unnecessarily or hurriedly. He did not expect that parliament would listen to the petitioners, yet he determined to await the result.

At the first meeting of the petitioners at the Feather's Tavern, July 17th, 1771,[2] with Lindsey in the chair, no more than twenty-four were present and the signatures to the petition did not number 250. As was natural, it had been drawn up by Archdeacon Blackburne. When he had first suggested the appeal, he had declared that the principle of the Reformation was that 'Holy Scripture contains all things necessary to salvation' and that on disputable points 'original protestant principle reserves to every man his right of private judgment'.[3] The 36th article of the Church of England enjoined 'all and every of these articles to be acknowledged, examined, and subscribed, as *agreeable to the word of God*'. Blackburne pointed out that this declaration was incompatible with 'the liberty wherewith Christ has made us free'. Now in the petition, the petitioners claimed that they had 'natural right' as well as Protestant principle, 'to judge in searching the scriptures, each man for himself, what may or may not be proved thereby'. This invaluable privilege was injured by the laws of subscription 'whereby your

[1] Rutt, i. 82.   [2] Ibid. i. 144.   [3] Blackburne, *Works*, vii, pp. 3 and 4.

petitioners are required to acknowledge certain articles and confessions of faith and doctrine, drawn up by fallible men, to be all and every of them, agreeable to the said Scriptures'. 'Your petitioners therefore pray that they may be relieved from such an imposition upon their judgement, and be restored to their undoubted right as Protestants of interpreting Scripture for themselves, without being bound by any human explications thereof, or required to acknowledge, by subscription or declaration, the truth of any formulary of religious faith and doctrine whatsoever, beside Holy Scripture itself'.[1] At the same time relief was sought for young men entering the universities. The petition was confided to the care of Mr. John Lee, a native of Leeds and, when on holiday, a member of Priestley's congregation, who subsequently became Solicitor-General in Lord Rockingham's ministry. It was presented to Parliament by Sir William Meredith, member for Liverpool. Lord North hoped to evade the issue by paying no attention to the petition, but his wisdom was not to the liking of the University of Oxford. Refusal to receive the petition was moved by Sir Roger Newdigate, member for the University. He alone spoke in favour of the Thirty-Nine Articles, the remaining opponents of the petition favouring the *status quo* because it was the *status quo*. The most illustrious of these was Edmund Burke. According to Lindsey he 'declaimed most violently against us in a long speech, but entirely like a Jesuit, and full of popish ideas'. 'Can it be true?' continued Mr. Lindsey; 'I hope not; but it is said, and suspected, that this man spoke the sentiments of his patron, Lord Rockingham. The persuasion, however, does my Lord Marquis no good in the esteem of judicious men.'[2] But Burke's opposition seems reasonable enough

---

[1] Blackburne, *Works*, vii. 16.   [2] Belsham, p. 39.

to-day. He pointed out that the willingness to sign assent to Scripture was assenting 'to a doctrine as contrary to your natural understanding, and to your rights of free inquiry, as those who require your conformity to any one article whatsoever'. Besides, what was meant by the Bible?

'The Bible is a vast collection of different treatises; a man who holds the divine authority of one, may consider the other as merely human. What is his canon? The Jewish—St. Jerome's—that of the Thirty-Nine Articles—Luther's?—Therefore, to ascertain Scripture you must have one Article more; and you must define what that Scripture is which you mean to teach. There are, I believe, very few who, when scripture is so ascertained, do not see the absolute necessity of knowing what general doctrine a man draws from it, before he is sent down authorized by the State to teach it as a pure doctrine, and receive a tenth of the produce of our lands'.[1]

Here Burke has gone to the very centre of the problem, not only of the church of the eighteenth but of the twentieth century. Establishment and freedom cannot go together. If variety of opinion is to be allowed, some sort of congregationalism must follow, for it is certainly monstrous that a man should reside in a parish, benefit by its emoluments, and use a liturgy, or teach doctrines utterly repugnant to his congregation. On the other hand, Burke did not appreciate the struggle after truth that characterized the petitioners.

'I will not enter into the question how much truth is preferable to peace. Perhaps truth may be far better.

[1] Burke, *Speech on Acts of Uniformity*.

But as we have scarcely ever the same certainty in the one that we have in the other, I would, unless the truth were evident indeed, hold fast to peace, which has in her company charity, the highest of the virtues.'[1]

In opposing the petition Lord North stated that should the Nonconformist ministers seek relief from signing the articles he would favour them. Among those who supported the petition were Thomas Pitt, Lord Chatham's nephew, and Sir George Savile, member for Yorkshire, one of the most upright and respected members who has graced any House of Commons. His speech, Lee declared, 'was one of the best that was ever delivered in that House.'[2] When the House divided, the numbers for not receiving the petition were 217, for receiving it 71. The result was expected, but the petitioners were pleasantly surprised by the size of their minority. Though the question was not dropped immediately it made no further progress, and the articles of the Church of England still chain its ministers, in spite of the progress of knowledge, to the intellectual position of the sixteenth century.

Lindsey, seeing now that there was no chance of relaxation, determined to leave the Church, and in December 1773 he resigned his parish of Catterick. The following April, encouraged and helped by Priestley, he opened the first avowedly Unitarian chapel in Essex Street, Strand, on the site where Essex Hall now stands.

Priestley had watched the Anglican application to Parliament with interest. The whole idea of an establishment was repugnant to him.

'You must permit us Dissenters', he wrote to Lindsey, 'however, who are not used to the idea even of *spiritual* superiors, to smile at your scheme, as an

[1] Burke, *Speech on Acts of Uniformity.*   [2] Belsham, p. 36.

application to the powers of this world for a reformation in the business of religion. As a disciple of a Master whose kingdom is not of this world, I should be ashamed to ask anything of temporal powers, except mere peace and quietness, which, being temporal blessings, they may bestow. The more I think of an application to such an House of Commons, or such a Parliament as ours, on the subject of religion, the more does the absurdity of it strike me.'[1]

After their defeat Lindsey at once urged the Dissenters to hurry on their application for relief from subscription. Priestley feared that too many applications would alarm the statesmen. Yet 'I rejoice in every thing that occasions a discussion of such important subjects'.[2] The Bill was actually introduced on April 3rd and Priestley attended the debate. He wrote to Lindsey:

'I snatch a moment to inform you that I am just returned from the House of Commons, where the motion to bring in a Bill to excuse Dissenting ministers and schoolmasters from an obligation to subscribe any of the Thirty-Nine Articles was carried triumphantly.

'Sir Harry Houghton made the motion, and Sir G. Savile seconded it. It was opposed by Sir Roger Newdigate, and Dolben, and the elder of the Foxes, but they spoke miserably indeed. Mr. Burke spake admirably in our favour, and Mr. Onslow, Mr. Montagu, and several others, also spake well.

'I am sorry, however, that our success was carried in such a manner as bodes your petition no good. Almost all the speakers laid great stress on the difference between your case and ours, contending for a strict establishment and a large toleration.

[1] Rutt, i. 160.   [2] Ibid. i. 162.

'The bishops at first favoured us, then violently opposed, and now seem to acquiesce. Lord North was not present, and I believe the ministry wished us well.'[1]

This time Burke spoke in favour of religious liberty, and denounced those Dissenters less liberal than the applicants, who opposed the petition. The Bill was defeated in the House of Lords by the influence of the bishops encouraged by the King.

Priestley was not a promoter of the petition, for, as he remarked himself, 'the man who takes the lead in any body of men whatever must be a man of more caution and prudence than I can boast.' Neither would he nor any of the rational Dissenters profit by the repeal of the subscription,[2] since the Unitarians as well as Roman Catholics were particularly exempted from the benefits of the Toleration Act. From the time of Calamy they had neither subscribed nor had any authority thought fit to demand it. Religious persecution was on the decline, and the dominant party contented itself with the exclusion of its opponents from the Universities and the curtailment of their civil rights. Still the Toleration Act was not yet a hundred years old, and there was enough irritation between the Established Church and the Dissenters for the latter to wish a firmer basis for their safety than mere indifference. But as an onlooker Priestley criticized the application. He objected to the petitioners praying as Christians for what they should stand forth 'in the character of *men* and ask'.[3] If the petitioners must call themselves Christians let them at least include all Christians 'and ask for the repeal of all the other laws which subject any Christians to pains and penalties, as well as that which is usually called the *Act of Toleration*'.[4]

---

[1] Rutt, i. 164. [2] Subscription to thirty-six of the thirty-nine Articles.
[3] *Works*, xxii. 442. [4] Ibid. xxii. 443–4.

Arians and Socinians, as well as Arminians, should be
included within the circle of toleration.

Priestley wanted ecclesiastical reformation. He wanted
the Test Act abolished, and the obligation removed
which lay upon 'members of parliament, civil and
military officers, physicians and doctors of music to
subscribe to the Thirty-Nine Articles of the Church of
England'.[1] It was bad enough for the State to maintain
authorized teachers of religion, but it was worse that they
should make part of the legislature. 'Indeed the temporal
power of the bishops of Rome is not, in its own nature,
more absurd than the temporal power of the bishops of
England.'[2] In all these matters the good of the State
should be first considered and 'both *ecclesiastical* and
civil duties would be better performed, if those functions
were entirely detached from one another'.[2] Politicians
should also see whether there was 'any utility in ecclesiastical establishments at all'. Free discussion of the constitution cannot harm the State. Great advantage would
accrue to it should its members learn 'to think with freedom, to speak and write with boldness, to suffer in a good
cause with patience, to begin to act with caution, but to
proceed with vigour'.[3] Danger to the constitution lay
rather in restriction than in freedom. 'It is chiefly when
men are restrained from expressing themselves in words,
that they ever think of having recourse to blows. When
the current is not allowed a free outlet, it is no wonder
that it swells and bears down all before it.'[3]

Extracts from his writings had been read by the Bishop
of Llandaff in the House of Lords as evidence of Priestley's
heresy. The accusation of idolatry which he had brought
against the Church of England had caused an outburst of
anger. He now brought the accusation once more and

[1] Ibid. xxii. 451.   [2] Ibid. xxii. 453.   [3] Ibid. xxii. 455.

foretold that the Church would not escape punishment in those 'days of vengeance' that he believed to be fast approaching.[1]

The most violent opposition to the Bill came from some of the Dissenters. They showed themselves to be 'utter enemies to the toleration of any but themselves'.[2] The worst of these were the '*Methodists*, or those Dissenters who had lately been Methodists, and who, therefore, could not be supposed to be acquainted with the sentiments and wants of the *proper Dissenters*, by which I mean, in this case, the Dissenters of some standing.'[3]

The general outlook was bad. Orthodox Christianity must either resign its usurpations or be overthrown. The difficulty of reformation would probably end in catastrophe. 'The state of Europe is at this time critical and alarming, beyond what it was ever known to be before. The slightest attention cannot but discover the seeds of great and calamitous events in almost every kingdom of it, so that we must be upon the eve of great revolutions.'[4] Present systems of government are ridiculously expensive: most of the states are burthened with debts, 'yet this extreme poverty, and inability to go to war, it is probable, will not long be sufficient to preserve the precarious peace which we now enjoy.'[5]

In the summer of 1772 Price recommended Priestley to Lord Shelburne to fill the position of librarian. The older man wished to see the younger, whom he loved, better provided for.[6] Priestley hesitated some time before accepting, but Shelburne was importunate, and he at last yielded. Shortly before he had been disappointed, for he was asked to accompany Captain Cook, as naturalist, on his second voyage, and had even gone so far as to find

[1] *Works*, xxii. 459.   [2] Ibid. xxii. 479.   [3] Ibid. xxii. 480.
[4] Ibid. xii. 481.   [5] Ibid. xxii. 482.   [6] *Am. Philos. Soc. MSS.*

some one to take his place at Leeds, but his appointment was turned down, for, it is supposed, some clergymen on the Board of Longitude objected to his religious opinions. So when Shelburne was visiting Leeds in August he called on Priestley and pressed his offer. It was certainly very handsome. At Leeds he had received only a hundred guineas per annum and a house and now he was offered £250 and a house in Calne, and the promise of a certainty for life in the case of Shelburne's death or of a separation. Priestley had been very happy at Mill Hill, but the offer was too advantageous both for himself and his family to be refused. In the following summer he moved to Calne.

F

THE character of William Fitzmaurice, second Earl of Shelburne, successfully baffled contemporaries and has proved no less of an enigma to historian and biographer. Shelburne's ancestors had been for twenty generations lords of Kerry when his grandfather married Anne, 'a very ugly woman',[1] daughter of Sir William Petty, who had been by turns many things, and had acquired great wealth. On the failure of the male line, the Petty wealth and estates passed to John Fitzmaurice, fifth son of Anne, and in his favour was revived the Petty title of Shelburne.

William Fitzmaurice was born in 1737. After a very neglected education he joined the Army, serving first of all under General Wolfe, but not accompanying him on the expedition against Quebec. For his gallantry at Minden and Kloster-Kampen Fitzmaurice was rewarded by the appointment of aide-de-camp to the young king, George III. The following year he succeeded his father as Earl of Shelburne. Originally friend of Bute and Henry Fox, he quarrelled with both. For a short time he had served as President of the Board of Trade in Grenville's Ministry, but caring for neither the home nor colonial policy of his colleagues, he had resigned. Choosing Pitt for his leader, he kept apart from the Rockinghams, and in the Chatham Ministry served as Secretary of State.

Chatham's strange illness during the years 1767 and 1768 made all intercourse with him impossible, and, finding himself opposed to the rest of his colleagues on nearly every point, Shelburne first of all ceased to attend Cabinet meetings, and finally resigned in October 1768.

[1] Fitzmaurice, p. 2.

Henceforward, to the end of the American War, Shelburne was one of the rival Leaders of the Opposition.

Unlike so many ill-educated persons of wealth and position, Shelburne tried to remedy his own lack of early education by making use of the information of others. At a later period Rayneval remarked to Vergennes that Shelburne's friends and entourage did him honour.[1] At twenty-four, Blackstone had confided in him his desire to modernize University education. Richard Price, whom Shelburne first met in 1769, was ready to advise his friend on questions of finance. Benjamin Franklin was also of his circle. But in the 'sixties and 'seventies the most important of Shelburne's friends were Barré and Dunning. Isaac Barré, son of a Huguenot refugee who had settled at Dublin, had been offered a thousand a year by Garrick if he would go on the stage. He had preferred the Army and had been at Wolfe's side when he fell on the Heights of Abraham.[2] A bullet lodged in his cheek distorted his features at the same time as it bore witness to his sufferings in his country's cause, sufferings an ungrateful King did his best to forget, for George III is supposed to have hated Barré second only to Wilkes. Barré is said to have been unrivalled as an opposition orator and none opposed North's Ministry more effectively than he did.

Dunning had risen to fame for his arguments against the legality of general warrants and his defence of Wilkes. For some time in the Grafton Ministry he held the position of Solicitor-General, though royal dislike barred his way to taking silk. But in 1770 he resigned after first attacking the Government, and was one of Shelburne's most faithful supporters in opposition. It was he who appeared for Franklin before the Privy Council in 1774,

[1] Ibid. ii. 182.   [2] Ibid. i. 96.

and in 1780 he made himself for ever famous by moving the resolution 'That the influence of the Crown has increased, is increasing, and ought to be diminished'. Both Barré and Dunning sat for Shelburne's pocket borough of Calne.

Though no proofs were ever forthcoming, Shelburne had the reputation among his contemporaries, and the tradition has survived, that he was lacking in honesty and straightforwardness. He was called Malagrida, and the Jesuit of Berkeley Square, nicknames, which, once given, were sure to stick. Some defect of character he must have had, for there can be no doubt that he was difficult to get on with, perhaps the result of never having gone to school, so that he had not learnt to rub shoulders with others. As we shall see, Priestley's connexion came to an end and the friendship never revived. With Charles Fox, Shelburne quarrelled at a time when the Government of the country depended on them. Barré parted company with Shelburne after twenty years of friendship. Bentham thought himself misled by some remarks of his patron, and Pitt, having first held office in Shelburne's Cabinet, never offered him any position whatsoever when in the following year George III asked him to form a Government.

In his travels with Barré through Italy and France in 1771 Shelburne had met in Paris most of its famous men, and many of the encyclopaedists. He had made the acquaintance of Turgot, not yet Controller-General but Intendant of the Limousin, of the Baron d'Holbach, and of the Abbé Morellet, most important of all for his influence on the development of Shelburne's thought. Morellet had been the schoolfellow of Turgot and of Lomenie de Brienne. His translation of the works of Beccaria and his writings on French criminal law had awakened his countrymen to the evils of their penal system. Also an economist, he taught the doctrine of free trade before *The Wealth of Nations* made knowledge of sound economic theory possible to men of average ability. Morellet became close friend to Shelburne, whom he visited in England and with whom he corresponded throughout the rest of Shelburne's life, for he survived all the horrors of the French Revolution, though he saw most of his friends fall around him, and lived until 1819. Shelburne, disciple first of Morellet and later of Adam Smith, was thus the first English statesman to hold free trade principles.

Shelburne favoured Parliamentary as well as economic reform. Later in the century, as friend of Bentham and Romilly, he helped to encourage reform of all kinds. During the dark days of fear and persecution in England that followed on the outbreak of the French Revolution he remained true to his liberalism, and did not allow himself to be driven by French excesses into the camp of English reaction.

Like so many of his Whig contemporaries, Shelburne loved the country and was never happier than when embellishing, with the help of the Adams brothers, his house of Bowood and when laying out the gardens with 'Capability' Brown. Like the true patron of learning that he was, he collected rare manuscripts and books, which his heedless descendants sold, but which, fortunately enough, were bought by the British Museum with the first grant of public money which it ever had to spend. Not only did Shelburne collect old masters, but he bought the pictures of contemporaries for the special object of encouraging art.

The best description of Bowood life is to be found in Bentham's letters. Unfortunately Bentham's visits to

Bowood did not begin until the year after Priestley's departure. By that time Shelburne had remarried, and though his aunt, Lady Arabella Denny, had acted as hostess on occasions, the charm of the later period, which, from Bentham's picture, seems to have largely depended on the ladies of the household, must have been absent. On his arrival Bentham was rather taken aback for 'when my Lord came in, he ran up to me, and touched one of my cheeks with his, and then the other . . . I should have been still better satisfied if he had made either of the ladies his proxy.'[1] In Priestley's day there was no Lady Shelburne, nor Miss Vernon, nor Miss Caroline Fox with whom to play billiards or chess. We may surmise that, though Shelburne entertained, it was not in the same way as during the lifetime of his first wife, the writer of the charming diary partially reproduced in Lord Fitzmaurice's *Life of Shelburne*, nor as later, after his marriage with Lady Louisa Fitzpatrick, sister of Lady Holland and of Richard Fitzpatrick, Charles Fox's friend.

Priestley tells us that his position, though nominally that of librarian, and superintendent of the education of Lord Fitzmaurice, and of 'Mr. William Petty, whose tutor, Mr. Jervis, was also a dissenting minister, was really that of literary companion to Lord Shelburne'. Whatever the demands of his patron, Priestley had more time than ever he had before to do what he liked; only out of regard for Shelburne, he refrained from political publications. So he could give his time to his favourite pursuits of science, metaphysics, and theology, though some of his publications on the last two subjects were supposed to have done his patron as much harm as would have been done by political writing.

The Priestleys settled in a pleasant house on the

1 Bentham, *Works*, x. 90.

Castle field at Calne, and there another child was born to them, whom at Lord Shelburne's request they called Henry. Here Priestley entertained on his own account, always having, as he said, 'a bed for a friend'. He received visits from his fellow Dissenting ministers and scientists, perhaps taking the latter along to stir up the mud in the river Calne, where his memory and this habit are perpetuated in *Doctor's Pond*. In the summer of 1774 he accompanied Shelburne on a tour to the continent. During the winter months Priestley lived with Shelburne in London, leaving his family in the country. On these visits he stayed at Shelburne House, later renamed Lansdowne House, which Shelburne had bought partly built from the Earl of Bute, and had finished with the help of Adam.

Priestley, no doubt, led very much his own life. He would mix in Dissenting circles, visiting his friend Lindsey, now established in Essex Street, sometimes on Sundays taking the service for him. Here he met Mrs. Rayner, who, though 'nearly allied in blood to the illustrious House of Percy, esteemed it a still greater honour to be the friend and fellow worshipper of Mr. and Mrs. Lindsey'.[1] She was wealthy and became Priestley's benefactress as well as Lindsey's. Naturally Priestley saw much of Price, as Whig, Dissenter, and Fellow of the Royal Society, and he would attend all meetings of the Society, and exchange information of discoveries and expectations. Apparently he met Wesley on several occasions, and though Wesley deplored his theology, the meetings were pleasant enough, and Priestley remembered that 'Mr. Wesley himself has often declared in the most public manner, in my hearing, that methodism had nothing to do with any particular religion, that the

[1] Epitaph in Bunhill Fields, quoted in *Inquirer*, 18 Aug. 1928.

end of all religion was good morals and that every man who had this object was his friend'.[1] There were also dinners at Johnson's, the publisher, at his house in St. Paul's Churchyard, where Priestley would meet, besides his Dissenting friends, such diverse characters as Cowper, Horne Tooke, Fuseli, and William Blake, and perhaps, at a later period, Tom Paine, Godwin, and Mary Wollstonecraft.[2] Nor must Benjamin Vaughan be forgotten, an old, if sometimes troublesome, pupil of Priestley's, but now intimate with Shelburne. The first garden strawberries cultivated in this country are said to have been grown by Vaughan from plants given him by Shelburne, which had been sent from Saratoga.[3]

The years Priestley spent in the service of Lord Shelburne were overshadowed by the American storm. From first to last, like any good Whig, Priestley sympathized with the colonists in opposition to the Crown. He considered the colonists just as much Englishmen as the inhabitants of this island,[4] and he saw danger both at home and abroad should George III's bid for arbitrary power succeed. Indeed, in all generations the Dissenter has been right to dread arbitrary power, for royalty has always in its heart suspected that James I's dictum, 'No bishop, no king,' might prove true. Benjamin Franklin, the most important American in England at this time, had been Priestley's intimate friend for many years, and both were members of the Club of Honest Whigs, as Franklin called it, that met at the London Coffee House. While Priestley spent his winters with Lord Shelburne in London, he tells us, scarcely a day passed by in which he and Franklin did not meet. Priestley and Burke went

---

[1] *Works*, xxv. 333. Introduction to Original Letters by the Rev. John Wesley.
[2] Gilchrist, *Life of Blake*, i. 92.
[3] Alger, *Englishmen in the French Revolution*. p. 91.
[4] *Electricity*, p. 231.

together to hear Franklin examined in the old Cockpit in Whitehall, on the Massachusetts petition, an occasion which was never forgotten, for it was then that Wedderburn, the Solicitor-General, attacked the colonial agent with gross invective, to the delight and amusement of His Majesty's Most Honourable Privy Council. When all efforts to prevent the quarrel ending in bloodshed had fallen through, and Franklin was determined to return home, he spent the last day before he sailed from morning till night in Priestley's company. Together they read the American papers, Franklin directing Priestley what should be sent for insertion in the English press. They never again met, but they managed somehow or other, in spite of war, to write to each other, a correspondence which was possibly responsible for the supposition that Lord Shelburne was in communication with the enemy. Looking on the colonists as brothers, and himself as their partisan, there was nothing treasonable in such correspondence, and indeed one of these letters was entrusted to the care of Major Carleton, brother to the Governor of Quebec.

Priestley did not object to the idea of American independence. We find him forwarding Price's pamphlet on Civil Liberty.

'By the same hand (Major Carleton's) you will receive a most excellent pamphlet by Dr. Price, which, if anything can, will, I hope, make some impression upon this infatuated nation. An edition of a thousand has been nearly sold in two days. But when Ld. G. Germaine is at the head of affairs, it cannot be expected that anything like *reason* or *moderation* should be attended to. Everything breathes *rancour* and *desperation*, and nothing but absolute impotence will stop their proceedings. We therefore look upon a final separation from you as a certain and speedy event. If anything can unite us, it must be the immediate adopting of the measures proposed by Lord Shelburne and mentioned in Dr. Price's pamphlet.

'As however, it is most probable you will be driven to the necessity of governing yourselves, I hope you will have wisdom to guard against the rock that we have fatally split upon; and make some better provision for securing your natural rights against the incroachment of power, in whomsoever placed. . . . The Club of *Honest Whigs*, as you justly call them, think themselves much honoured by you having been one of them, and also by your kind remembrance of them. Our zeal in the good cause is not abated. You are often the subject of our conversation.'[1]

Almost a year passed before Franklin answered that letter, and by then he was representing the Thirteen United States in Paris.

'I suppose you would like to know something of the state of affairs in America,' he wrote. 'In all probability we shall be much stronger the next campaign than we were in the last; better armed, better disciplined, and with more ammunition. When I was in camp before Boston, the army had not five rounds of powder to a man. This was kept a secret, even from our own people. The world wondered that we so seldom fired a cannon. We could not afford it, but we may now make powder in plenty.

'To me it seems, as it has always done, that this war must end in our favour, and in the ruin of Britain, if she do not speedily put an end to it. An English gentleman here the other day, in company with some

[1] Feb. 13th, 1776, Priestley to Franklin. *Am. Philos. Soc. MSS.*

French, remarked, that it was folly in France not to make war immediately. And, *in England,* replied one of them, *not to make peace.*'[1]

After war had broken out, Priestley, along with Dr. Price and others, did what he could to help the American prisoners, whom the Government, though hesitating to treat fully as traitors, did not altogether recognize as prisoners of war.

Many, indeed, must have been the unhappy hours through which the friends of America passed. The hopefulness of the Government with its solid majority in Parliament and the apathy of the people only increased their gloom.

In the summer of 1776 Shelburne was again on the continent and Priestley informed him of what was going on at home. On September 11th he wrote:

'As far as I can collect, all things wear the same aspect here that they did when your Lordship left us, the country at large is indifferent, and the ministry, at least before the late check at Charleston, equally sanguine. Dr. Frampton showed me a letter he had just received from Lord Suffolk, in which, after mentioning his own health, he said he expected very soon to have news of much more importance to all Englishmen than the health of any individual. This was about three weeks ago, but his expectations have not yet been fulfilled, and Genl. Howe's continuing so long before New York, without attempting anything of consequence, looks as if he does not find the enterprise so easy as he, or those who sent him, had imagined.

'Mr. Lindsey, whose intelligence is generally pretty accurate, says he is informed, from the very best

[1] Rutt, i. 297. Jan. 27th, 1777.

authority, that there is an irreconcilable difference between Ld. Gower and Mr. Rigby. Whether this is likely to have any effect on public measures your Lordship will be able to judge.

'For my own part, I endeavour to think as little as I possibly can (which, however, is not very little) of *Politics*, and apply myself to pursuits in which I meet with less cause of chagrin, and in which I hope I am not uselessly employed.'[1]

It is not very possible to trace any very decided action by Priestley in politics during these years. Undoubtedly he came more and more to share the opinions of the Rockingham party. Sir George Savile was an old friend. Charles Fox seems at this time to have been friendly with both sections of the opposition, and Priestley probably met him frequently at Lord Shelburne's, for in later years he complained of Fox's bad manners as a young man 'when he spat on the carpet and hurt Lord Shelburne, who is a man of great neatness'.[2] Priestley was not in the least alarmed by the idea of independence, but Shelburne, on the other hand, while fully admitting the folly and the wrongfulness of the struggle, opposed it. On March 5th, 1778, he declared 'he would never consent that America should be independent', and he considered that as soon as the colonies were lost, 'the sun of Great Britain is set, and we shall no longer be a powerful or a respectable people, the moment that the independency of America is agreed to by our government'.

'He did not mean,' he is reported to have said, 'that he never would agree to a connexion with the colonies as independent states: circumstances might create a necessity for such a submission, though they could not

[1] *Bowood MSS.*   [2] *Early Life of Samuel Rogers*, p. 245.

justify the folly or treachery of our administration, which should reduce them and the nation to so abject a situation: but he asserted that, when the day came, on which American independence should be acknowledged by that House, he trusted, that House would, with one voice, call for justice on those who should be the occasion of so fatal a necessity.'[1]

Shelburne advised continuing the war merely as a naval war, holding on to a few towns on the seaboard of the colonies until their alliance with France should be broken, and an equitable union between the colonies and the mother country once more established, a policy which just possibly might have succeeded.

On the seventeenth Shelburne again spoke. The occasion was the debate on the royal message notifying the House of the acknowledgement by France of the colonies as independent states. Shelburne held that the declaration of the French ambassador made war inevitable, but were we, he asked, prepared for such an event? 'Without fleets, without armies, without allies, and without resources, what was to be done?' Government must be mended and corruption cease. 'Thus by lightening the pressure upon the people, they would have power to exert themselves; their ancient spirit would be revived, and entering into the war with cheerfulness and alacrity, they would pursue it with vigour.' . . . He concluded with declaring that he was an advocate for peace, if it could be procured with honour, which he did not think possible.[2]

About this time Shelburne was approached by Lord North in the hope of persuading him to come into, and thereby strengthen, the ministry. William Eden, one of

---

[1] *Parliamentary History.*　　　　　[2] Ibid.

the commissioners appointed to bring about the recon-
ciliation with the colonies, was first sent to try his skill as
peacemaker on Shelburne. 'At a quarter past seven,' he
reported, 'I called on Dr. Priestley who introduced me to
Lord Shelburne and left us.'[1] This visit, as well as the two
speeches, aroused the librarian's anxiety as to the part
which his patron was about to play. The following letter
shows on the one hand how little servile Priestley was in
relation to his employer, but on the other how little he
was in his confidence, in spite of the fact that he was used
to introduce the Government negotiator.

'My Lord,
      Considering the very great obligations I am under
to your Lordship, I think it my duty, painful as the
discharge of it is to me, faithfully to represent to your
Lordship the manner in which several persons, friends
of liberty and of their country, and also of your Lordship personally, are impressed by your Lordship's
late speech in the House of Lords, and the present
alarming state of public affairs; especially as they are
sentiments that are entertained by many others, and, I
am confident, will be adopted by such as are the most
truly respectable part of every nation, but whose
opinions and wishes are generally little considered,
because they give no disturbance to any administration.
When I say that the Bishop of St. Asaph[2] and Dr. Price
are of the number, your Lordship will know perfectly
what kind of men I mean. How far their opinions
should weigh with your Lordship, it is not for me to say.
      'From the general complexion and turn of your
Lordship's speech, they are apprehensive that in conjunction with Lord Chatham, whose speech upon a

[1] Russell, *Fox*, p. 181.   [2] Jonathan Shipley (1714–88).

former occasion was similar to your Lordship's, you are about to give your aid to the king in the last and most desperate of a train of measures, that cannot but end in the utter humiliation and ruin of the country; especially considering the representation your Lordship gave of the weak state of the nation, and the facility of an invasion from France.

'They think that a war with France is neither necessary or just, and that could we have the true magnanimity and wisdom to join with France, in acknowledging the independence of America, it would utterly disappoint and disconcert the French counsels, gain the good will and good wishes of America, and effectually detach them from an alliance with France in case of war; a war which, if entered upon by France in those circumstances, would be on our part *strictly* defensive, and in which there would be the hearty concurrence of all ranks of men amongst us. Whereas a French war in support of the independence of America will be considered as a sequel and part of the *American war* by the true friends not only of America, but of the liberties and real interests of this country, and therefore their wishes will not go along with it.

'A rigorous inquiry into the conduct of the present ministry, and the exemplary punishment of the most guilty of them, together with the thorough reformation of abuses in government, and especially the diminution of the enormous influence of the crown, are objects in which your Lordship has always hitherto taken the lead, and which they hope your Lordship will not lose sight of, or pursue with less vigour, because they are now, (though late) adopted by the friends of Lord Rockingham.

'I promise your Lordship that I shall not often

trouble you with my political opinions. This much I thought right as a proof of the proper attachment with which I am,

> My Lord, your Lordship's most faithful, humble, servant
> J. Priestley.

Shelburne House, March 20th, 1778.'[1]

But Priestley's fears for the consistency and honour of his patron were groundless, for Shelburne only considered coming in on his own terms, and not those of the king. 'Lord Chatham,' he said, 'must be the dictator', and both the Duke of Grafton and Lord Rockingham should be included. The king was furious with Shelburne's proposals. 'His language', wrote George III to his Prime Minister, 'is so totally contrary to the only ground on which I could have expected the service of that perfidious man, that I need not enter on it.'[2]

At this time the Rockinghams could not have come in with Shelburne, for they were opposed to him on the principle of American Independence. Like Priestley's friends they wished to take the wind out of the bellicose French sails by the acknowledgement of Independence, a policy which was sound enough in itself but, unfortunately, outside the range of practical politics as neither king nor people were yet fully educated to the idea in the hard school of military disaster. Priestley was wrong in believing that the French War would be considered merely as a sequel to the American. The treachery of the French was decried, and many an officer who had refused to fight against his fellow countrymen in America was ready to take service once more against the hereditary enemy.

---

[1] *Bowood MSS.*   [2] Fitzmaurice, ii. 17.

Priestley does not say much in his letters about the war and in his one reference to the combined French and Spanish fleets being in the Channel, he gives no account of his feelings nor of those of his neighbours at the nearness of the enemy.

In 1780 Shelburne and Priestley parted company. It is difficult to be sure of the exact cause of separation, probably there were many reasons. Perhaps the newly-wedded Lord Shelburne no longer wished for the intimacy of his librarian and literary companion. Shelburne did not care for controversial divinity, and he may have found his librarian too engrossed in this subject. Politically they disagreed and, as we have seen, Priestley did not hesitate to lecture his patron when he thought his political wisdom inadequate. It may have been that Shelburne, aspiring to the government, feared he should be compromised by Priestley's views and correspondence with Franklin. And then there is Benjamin Vaughan's testimony in regard to some of Priestley's publications. 'When he was with Lord L.', wrote Vaughan to his brother, John, in their American exile, 'I could only stop a publication for six months, though it was to hurt his patron with the public and the court, appear when it would.'[1] Whatever the cause, it was intimated to Priestley that Shelburne thought of providing for him on his Irish establishment, but Priestley preferred that the parting should be according to the original agreement; he therefore left Lord Shelburne, receiving from him an annuity of £150 for the rest of his life.

Shortly afterwards, on visiting London, Priestley wished to call on his old patron, but he was given to understand that Lord Shelburne did not wish to receive

---

[1] *Belloc Lowndes MSS.*, Oct. 27th, 1799—Shelburne was by then Lord Lansdowne.

him. At a later period, Shelburne, by then Marquis of
Lansdowne and with his political career a thing of the
past, wished to renew the friendship, but Priestley declined.

Whatever may have been the cause of separation, and
whoever was to blame, Priestley was indebted to Lord
Shelburne for seven years of comparative ease in which
he pursued his own favourite studies of metaphysics,
theology, and chemistry. He had moved in a much larger
sphere of society than that which usually comes the way
of a Dissenting minister, and through Shelburne had met
most of the distinguished men of the day. But a dependent
position is not always the most comfortable, and perhaps
it was just as well for Priestley that it should now come
to an end.

CHAPTER VI

TOUR ON THE CONTINENT

Autumn 1774

IN the second year of his engagement with Lord Shelburne, Priestley accompanied his patron on a tour of
the continent. This was the only occasion on which he
crossed the Channel. He has left an account of his journey
in three letters written to Lord Fitzmaurice, and his
brother William Petty. These two must have been preco-
cious children to have appreciated such letters, for at this
time Lord Fitzmaurice was not yet nine, and his brother
was three years younger. Taking their own coach and
cook with them, the travellers set out in August; crossing
the Channel at Calais they went by way of St. Omer,
Aire, and Bethune to Lille; Priestley wrote his observations
to the six-year-old 'Mr. Petty'. He thought the towns
better built than those at home but the furniture 'though
it has, in some respects, the air of great magnificence, is
in general ill made and not elegant; most things finished
in a manner that we should be ashamed of in England'.
He reports to the child the improvements noticed in the
cultivation as they got farther away from Calais.

'It seemed to be much superior to the generality of
English husbandry; but we have yet seen no inclosures,
and hardly any grass or meads, cows or sheep; these
being fed in places where the soil is not so rich. At
Bethune we were amused as we went through the
market with a sight of a number of the slenderest and
leanest pigs we had ever seen. They might almost have
been taken for greyhounds. The horses we have seen
are, in general, small, lean, and not at all handsome;
but, notwithstanding, very active, and do their business

very well. You would have smiled if you had been with us this morning, and seen, as I did, dogs drawing little carts with very considerable loads, and men drawing sedan chairs mounted on wheels. By this means, however, people are very well carried, and one man does the work of two with us.

'All the way we have come, we were surprised at the prodigious quantity of tall, fine beans, which are all standing, and especially with the plantations of tobacco and poppies, which are not cultivated in England. The tobacco was very green, and looked exceedingly beautiful; the poppies were all reaped and formed into sheaves or ricks. We could not imagine what use so much poppy seed could be, but upon inquiry we were informed that they get a great deal of oil from them, and that the many windmills we saw in the neighbourhood were all employed to press that oil, which is used for lamps.

'Though you are not a man of gallantry, yet, as you are an observer of human nature, I must tell you what has struck me most relating to the women we have seen. Many of them, even those who are well dressed, walk in the streets in slippers, without anything to cover the heel; so that, except the toe, the whole foot is seen as they walk, which to me, who never saw the like before, looked slatternly and indelicate. Almost all the women are dressed in what we call a French night-cap, which almost covers their cheeks; and we saw a great number of country women going to and from the market at Bethune, many of them in carts, with their heads dressed particularly neat; but not one of them had any hat to screen them from the sun or rain; nor have we seen one woman with a hat on since we left England. By this means they soon get sunburned and look ugly, while the men wear very large hats and save their faces. Instead of cloaks, the women of all ranks have a square piece of cloth or stuff which they throw over their shoulders or their heads at pleasure; and sometimes it is so large as to reach almost to their feet. Betwixt Lisle [*sic*] and Ghent, which we reached on Saturday, the country women were provided with straw bonnets, which, though not very elegant, must be very convenient. All the better sort of people, men as well as women, when they walk out in the sun or the rain, hold an umbrella in their hands, and sometimes one of them will serve for two persons. A number of these umbrellas have a very pretty appearance in a street, especially as they are of different colours, and the fashion of them is elegant; but they would by no means do in the streets of London, or any crowded place; for they necessarily take up a good deal of room.

'At Lisle, you, as having a military turn, would have received great pleasure from what was not only irksome, but a cause of a good deal of pain to me. This was a review of a regiment of French soldiers in compliment to your papa. They did not fire, but they performed a variety of new and very useful evolutions lately introduced by the King of Prussia. The pain that I felt on the occasion did not arise from any consideration of the mischief that this new discipline might enable the French to do us in any future war, but from a cold that I got at the time, which affected my teeth very much.'[1]

From Lille, Shelburne and Priestley passed through Belgium, breaking the journey at Brussels, where they dined with the Duke D'Aremburg, and then passing

[1] Rutt, i. 238–40.

through Antwerp entered Holland at Rotterdam. The journal is continued in a letter to Lord Fitzmaurice.

'The whole of Austrian Flanders is highly cultivated and populous. The farm-houses seemed to be substantially good, and the poorest people we met, tolerably well clothed. Indeed, we have not yet seen any people so exceedingly shabby and wretched as the poor of Calne. It is something remarkable, however, that in this country the boys that beg on the wayside have the very same ridiculous custom of tumbling and standing on their heads that you will see at Studley, and which I have also seen in one part of Yorkshire. But here we once saw a girl standing on her head for this purpose. You may be assured that we did not encourage so much idleness and indecency by giving them anything, though the custom could not have been established, if others had not been diverted with it and countenanced it.

'This country has formerly produced very excellent painters, especially the celebrated Rubens; and though (which is very remarkable) they can boast of no painters at present, the rich and curious give immense sums for pictures to furnish their cabinets, and some make a gainful traffic of buying to sell again. A curious character of this kind we met with at Ghent, who took no little pains, and used a good deal of address, to take in your papa. We got a sight of his pictures overnight, and as he was very importunate, partly promised to see him again the next morning. However, as we were walking in the church the next morning, which was Sunday, we happened to pass by a confessional chair where he was confessing an old woman; and the moment he cast his eyes upon us, he gave us an intimation that he would be with us immediately; and so dispatching his penitent with a most indecent hurry, he presently joined us. It was then impossible to avoid going to his house, from whence we returned, truly pleased with many of his pictures; more with so curious a character; and most of all that we saw through his artifice, and did not contribute to gratify his covetousness at our expense.

'Another adventure of this kind we had an Antwerp. One of these trafficking connoisseurs shewed us a picture as an original of Rubens; and asked a prodigious great price for it. Our guide, who, no doubt, was in league with him, evouched it; but going immediately from thence to the house of a rich and whimsical canon, we saw the real original of the very same picture, the same guide conducting us. This canon also was a much greater curiosity himself than anything he had to shew. He had no real knowledge of anything he had got, but had a valet who shewed them; and we were told, that sometimes when such questions were asked, as he could not answer himself, he would send for his maid. Indeed, his valet made so very free, both with his master and us, as made anything of this kind very credible. This canon was very eager to hear everything about him admired, but affected to make a great secret of everything, and, in the bluntest and rudest manner, said *no* to almost every question your papa asked him about the management of his flowers, &c.; and though we particularly admired some fine peaches that he had got, he would not understand the hint so far as to desire our acceptance of one; and had we directly asked him for one, as your papa, for curiosity, had once thought of doing, I doubt not he would have again said *no*; which was a monosyllable that seemed to be very familiar to him. Two such characters as those of these canons can hardly be found except in such seclusion from the world, and such an independence on others [*sic*], as is peculiar to the Romish clergy.

'From Alost to Brussels we saw many hops, and, I think, finer than any we had seen as we travelled through Kent. The beer of this country is by no means so good as in England.'[1]

From Antwerp, Shelburne and Priestley went to Rotterdam. Holland does not seem to have attracted Priestley as much as we should have expected from his strong Protestantism. He was disappointed in the country and in the people. The usual places were visited, the magnificent tomb of the Prince of Orange at Delft, and the physic garden at Leyden. At Haarlem they heard the famous organ playing. They intended to go to Saardam (Zaandam), where most of the Dutch ships were built, and (did Priestley remember?) where Peter the Great had studied the art; but they were cheated by their guides, 'who after having pocketed the money for that tour, took us another and shorter way; and had our lives depended upon it, instead of the gratifying of our curiosity, I almost think those Dutchmen would have done just the same thing, and with the same coolness and self-applause. But, for the honour of human nature, I am willing to think we should not have been served so in any other country.'[2]

Amsterdam, which even to-day gives a better idea of maritime enterprise than any other town, seemed to Priestley an astonishing sight. 'Such number of ships is, I believe, no where else to be found in one place. The Town House also astonished me, both for the expense and the magnificence of that part of it which is always

[1] Rutt, i. 240–2.   [2] Ibid. i. 243.

open to everybody (being all cased with marble, disposed in excellent taste and exquisite workmanship), and for the noble suite and furniture of the rooms adapted to all kinds of public business.' [1]

But on the whole Amsterdam was a disappointment, and they left earlier than they had meant, going by boat to Utrecht where they met the cook and the coach.

'In this passage we were much amused with the view of the Dutch country houses, with which this canal (as also that which led from Delft to Leyden) was lined. Some of them were old-fashioned, dark, and gloomy retreats, suitable enough, in my opinion, for those who had amassed a fortune in such a manner as is generally ascribed to this industrious, but selfish people. But in others there was real elegance and good taste, with a general uniformity (especially in long straight vistas of trees, some covered and some open, and all most exactly cut and trimmed) amidst a very great and whimsical variety. Some of them must have been exceedingly expensive, and equal to those of very rich country gentlemen in England.

'On Friday we left Utrecht, intending to have reached Nimeguen before night; but we found the roads so intolerably heavy, that we were obliged to lodge at a small place called Grip; so we dined at Nimeguen the next day, and got to Cleef, in the King of Prussia's dominions, that night; taking leave, to our great satisfaction, of the country and people of Holland.

'Altogether, however, it must be allowed that Holland is a great curiosity, and well worth the transient visit of a statesman, or a philosopher, though it is certainly the last in which a man of a liberal turn of mind would choose to live.

[1] Ibid. i. 244.

'The people here are so much occupied with commerce, that agriculture is no object of attention with them. We hardly saw a single field of corn in Holland, all the ground being employed in pasture. But though the cattle do not look ill, the horses are not capable of much service, and the flesh of their oxen and sheep is a loose texture, and without flavour. This is owing, I suppose to the marshiness of their meadows, and the very bad water they are obliged to drink. Indeed, the whole country of Holland does not afford any water that a man can well drink. This circumstance, at least, furnishes them with an excuse for drinking wine and spirituous liquors in great quantities, and also for smoking tobacco, with which they almost poison everybody that comes near them. Indeed, I can hardly express how very low, beastly, and sordid, the manners of the common people in this country are. It is a thing very different from the roughness and brutality of some of the low-bred people of England. In Germany or France, as far as I can observe, neither of those characters, which are the disgrace of human nature, exists.

'Upon the whole, we were much disgusted with the people of Holland, and their manners; and were glad to get into the more open air, and more natural and agreeable manners of Germany.' [1]

They travelled up the Rhine as far as Strasburg, seeing all the things they ought to see, and of course meeting all the people they should meet. They travelled leisurely enough, driving in the coach, or walking as they preferred. Sometimes on these occasions going across country, they lost their way, as they did on the journey to Landau, when their carriage missed them and they

[1] Rutt, 244–5.

rambled many miles and did not arrive at the town till the gates were shut.

Priestley was much pleased with the cultivation of Alsace, which he thought resembled a rich garden.

'This look is much favoured by the variety of crops, and the division of the fields, being often distinguished by rows of vines. All our varieties of corn, turkey wheat, canary seed, hemp, pumpkins, kidney beans, vines, turnips, potatoes, tobacco, and many other things, all intermixed in long and narrow fields, makes a new and curious spectacle to an Englishman. The roads, and also many of the fields, are planted with fruit trees, especially the walnut trees, the fruit of which is used for making oil.

'The soil of this country, and especially Alsace, is so light that they generally plough with one horse, or cow, which they always yoke by the horns, which was the custom everywhere in our travels, except in Lorraine, where we saw some oxen yoked as with us. In Lorraine we frequently saw them ploughing with eight horses, and women either holding the plough or driving it. The wheat of Alsace is celebrated. At Strasburgh we had bread of the most exquisitely fine flavour I ever tasted; and at Nancy we were told that they cannot make such in France.'

Priestley was properly impressed by the zeal of the Lutheran clergy in catechizing children. At Luneville they saw the manufacture of porcelain which apparently was different to anything Priestley had seen before, for he called it 'curious'.[1]

At last Paris was reached. One suspects Priestley of insular prejudice; anyway he was not impressed by what he saw of Paris, where he says he was struck by nothing 'except

[1] Ibid. i. 248–9.

the spaciousness and magnificence of the public buildings; and to balance this, I was exceedingly offended with the narrowness, dirt, and stench, of almost all the streets'.[1] Bad and unsavoury as London was, Paris was even worse.

In the spring of this year Louis XV had died and was succeeded by his grandson. Turgot was installed as Controller-General. Reform was the order of the day, for, if philosophers were not kings, they were at least ministers. Priestley, writing to Lindsey, declared that the aims of the Government were freedom of commerce and universal peace. What greater could any ministry have? It was a period of hopefulness when all things appeared possible. Shelburne, a great English peer, and a reformer in the days when reform was the fashion, was naturally received into the most interesting circle of French society, and with him went Priestley. Morellet, a visitor to Bowood two years earlier, was a schoolfellow of Turgot, and of Lomenie de Brienne, Archbishop of Toulouse, immortalized in the pages of Carlyle.

We may suppose that Priestley met most of the Encyclopaedists, that he would dine at the hospitable table of the Baron D'Holbach whose house was known as the 'Café de l'Europe'. Probably he attended the salon of Mademoiselle de l'Espinasse, friend of D'Alembert, whom Shelburne had impressed on a previous visit. She was greatly taken by the English lord who wished to improve the lot of his tenants, and build their children schools, and who invited her to visit him in England.

Priestley was already renowned as a philosopher and naturally met other members of the scientific world. He dined with Lavoisier, chemist and farmer-general, whose scientific training had been so different from his. There he met the youthful Madame Lavoisier, her husband's

---

[1] Rutt, i. 250.

assistant in many of his labours, so different from Mrs. Priestley, who though excellent housewife, was little interested in the good doctor's activities.

At Lavoisier's table were collected all the prominent philosophers of Paris. Priestley spoke of his recent, but not fully understood discovery of oxygen, the importance of which he never fully realized, and mystified them all by translating red lead as 'plombe rouge' till Macquer came to his rescue with the suggestion that it was 'minium' he meant.[1] Lavoisier's claim to independent discovery is therefore invalid, but it was he who realized its importance and revolutionized thereby the whole science of chemistry.

To Priestley, a middle-class Nonconformist, the society he was now expected to move in was indeed strange. Protestantism was almost unknown, and where Catholicism did not prevail, infidelity held the field. 'I am here', wrote Priestley to Lindsey, 'in the midst of unbelievers, and even Atheists. I had a long conversation with one, an ingenious man, and good writer, who maintained seriously that man might arise, without any Maker, from the earth. They may despise me; I am sure I despise them.'[2] Many of his friends wore the outward garb of religion; Morellet was an abbé and officiated; so was John Hyacynthe De Magalhaens, of the family of the Discoverer, whom Priestley had already met in London. There in 1768 Magalhaens had been indicted with three other priests, by a Protestant reformer before the court of King's Bench, but Lord Mansfield and the other judges had put an end to this persecution by finding a flaw in the procedure.[3]

Ecclesiastical dignity did not always mean much to the

---

[1] *Doctrine of Phlogiston*, Appendix 3.   [2] Rutt, i. 254.
[3] Burton, *Challoner*, ii. 93–5.

cause of Christianity. At a later period Samuel Rogers heard Priestley relate at the Hackney Club that:

'When I was dining at Paris fifteen years ago at Turgot's table, M. de Chatelleux—Author of *Travels Through America*—in answer to an inquiry said that the two gentlemen opposite me were the Bishop of Aix and the Archbishop of Toulouse,[1] "but," said he, "they are no more believers than you or I." I assured him I was a believer; but he would not believe me; and Le Roi, the philosopher, told me that I was the only man of sense he knew that was a Christian. A young man of family called upon me and said, with tears of joy in his eyes, that he heard I was a believer. "Yes," said I, "but I am a great heretic, not such a believer as you." "Still," said he, "you are a believer." '[2]

We suspect that Priestley was not always ready to hide his displeasure and disapprobation. Morellet, in a letter to Shelburne of the following winter, wrote 'J'embrasse de tout mon cœur mon bon ami M. Priestley, quoiqu'il n'ait pas trouvé à Paris le *it is so,* que je veux obtenir un jour de master William,[3] et qu'il n'ait jamais voulu dire *there are some good things.*'[4] But despite Priestley's provincialism he won the esteem of Morellet, and probably of others. A few years later Morellet sent a young man to learn chemistry from Priestley, but hoped above all that he would learn from him 'la simplicité, la vérité, la vertu, qui valent encore mieux que toute sa physique, quelque excellente qu'elle soit'.[5]

Priestley, tiring of Paris, abandoned Shelburne to its delights and returned to England in the company of Magalhaens.

---

[1] Boisgelin de Cucé' and Lomenie de Brienne.
[2] *Early Life of Samuel Rogers,* p. 266.   [3] Shelburne's second son.
[4] Morellet, p. 63.   [5] Ibid., p. 111.

CHAPTER VII

SCIENTIFIC WORK [1]

PRIESTLEY, as we have seen, had written his first scientific work, the *History of Electricity*, while he was tutor at Warrington. Its publication was the occasion of his election to the Royal Society. He was asked by the Grand Duke of Tuscany to send him the best electrical machine that could be got. As some complained that the *History* was too difficult, he brought out in 1768 a *Familiar Introduction to the Study of Electricity*. In producing these two books he could find no one at hand to illustrate them with drawings of the various instruments, and consequently it was necessary for him to make the drawings himself. As he incurred difficulty in procuring any simple book of perspective, Priestley decided to meet this need, and used the information he had acquired in his *Familiar Introduction to the Theory and Practice of Perspective*. But his next really important scientific work was *An Account of the Discoveries relating to Vision, Light, and Colours*. It was published in 1772 by subscription, but in spite of the long list of respectable names that appears at the beginning, containing those of Burke, Charles Fox, Franklin (20 copies), Sir Joshua Reynolds, Wilkes, 'Jeremiah Bentham of Lincoln's Inn,' [2] and many members of both Houses of Parliament, the cost of production was not met by the sale, and Priestley was unable to continue his scheme for writing the complete history of all branches of experimental philosophy. Perhaps this was fortunate, as he now gave his attention to that branch in which he was to win immortality. His experiments on air, so he tells us, were begun because his first house at Leeds was next door to a public brewery and he amused himself

[1] This chapter largely follows *Thorpe*.   [2] Is this Jeremy or his father?

with the fixed air (carbon dioxide) he found made in the process of fermentation. Later, when he moved away from the brewery, he had to make the fixed air for himself. His first publication appeared in 1772 and was entitled *Directions for Impregnating Water with Fixed Air.* Natural mineral waters had long been known for their efficacious medicinal values, and William Brownrigg had already succeeded in making water similar to the Seltzer water; Priestley's method was much more successful. He is regarded as the father of soda-water for his methods rather than for the invention. This pamphlet was immediately translated into French. Through Sir George Savile it was brought to the notice of Lord Sandwich, then first Lord of the Admiralty, for it was believed the water would be good in treating sea scurvy. Priestley made the experiments before the College of Physicians. They recommended the use of the water and two battleships were fitted with the necessary apparatus. At a later period, when Priestley accompanied Shelburne to the continent, they passed by a spring of Seltzer water, but there was no time for experimenting beyond extinguishing a candle in the air.

The summer of 1772 was brightened, and Priestley's researches encouraged, by a visit to Leeds of Benjamin Franklin and Sir John Pringle, President of the Royal Society. 'You make me very happy', wrote Priestley to Franklin on June 13th, 'by the near prospect of seeing you and Sir John Pringle at Leeds. I shall be entirely at liberty to receive you, and I hope you will continue to stay as long as possible in the town and neighbourhood.' Priestley was already complaining of the cost of experiments and his lack of means. 'If I had studied *Poor Richard* in time, I should not have indulged myself in these expenses, but bad habits are not easily corrected. If, however, the passion be not kept up by considerable success, frugality, and an attention to a growing family, will, at length, get the better of experimenting, and then I shall write nothing but *Politics* or *Divinity*, to furnish the Bishop of Llandaff with more quotations for his invectives against the Dissenters.' [1]

Priestley's great fame as a chemist rests upon his six volumes on Air. The first volume appeared in 1774 and the last in 1786, but most of the experiments were made during the seven years he was in the service of Lord Shelburne. The first volume is appropriately dedicated to his patron and contains a lengthy preface. Priestley explained that the work must not be supposed to be perfect, for every publication of the kind needs must be incomplete, for 'the works of God are, like himself, infinite and inexhaustible'. Scientific discovery reminds him of 'Pope's description of travelling among the Alps, with this difference, that here there is not only a *succession*, but an *increase* of new objects and difficulties.

> So pleas'd at first the towering Alps we try,
> Mount o'er the vales, and seem to tread the sky,
> Th' eternal snows appear already past,
> And the first clouds and mountains seem the last.
> But those attain'd, we tremble to survey
> The growing labours of the lengthen'd way.
> Th' increasing prospect tires our wand'ring eyes,
> Hills peep o'er hills, and Alps on Alps arise!

Priestley can never resist the temptation of using his prefaces as gilding for a theological pill with which to dose his unbelieving scientific readers. He declares that the rapid progress of knowledge will extirpate all error and prejudice, and will put 'an end to all undue and

[1] *Am. Philos. Soc. MSS.*

H

usurped authority in the business of *religion*, as well as of *science*; and all the efforts of the interested friends of corrupt establishments of all kinds will be ineffectual for their support in this enlightened age; though, by retarding their downfall, they may make the final ruin of them more complete and glorious. It was ill policy in Leo the Xth to patronize polite literature. He was cherishing an enemy in disguise. And the English hierarchy (if there be any thing unsound in its constitution) has equal reason to tremble even at an air pump, or an electrical machine'. In France, Catholic by law but sceptical by the fashion of the day, part of this preface was suppressed. There never was a more honest scientist than Priestley. His intention, faithfully carried out, was to place all his mistakes and false suppositions before his reader, and show how they had led to true discoveries. Had Priestley been more a man of the world, had he possessed a little less of that simplicity and truthfulness that had won Morellet's esteem, his reputation as a chemist might have stood higher. Suppose he had only given those parts of his discoveries which had worked out successfully!

The first volume contained Priestley's earlier experiments made before his removal to Calne. Most important were the papers *Of Air in which a Candle or Brimstone has burnt out* (No. 2) and *Of Air infected with Animal Respiration and Putrefaction* (No. 4), complementary to each other. The Count de Salucé had claimed, in the memoirs of the Philosophical Society of Turin, that air vitiated by the burnings of candles could be restored by exposure to cold. Priestley found that this was not the case, but he discovered that the air was restored by a sprig of mint growing in it. But it is only in Volume 4 that he finally proved in the paper entitled 'Melioration of Air by the Growth of Plants' that the restoration of the air was due to the green matter of leaves and that it was dependent on sunlight.[1]

Priestley had been intrigued by an account in Hales's *Statistical Essays* of an experiment in which common air, and air generated from the Walton pyrites, by spirit of nitre, made a turbid red mixture. Priestley did not expect to see this phenomenon himself, supposing the Walton pyrites to be important, until Cavendish made the suggestion that the peculiar colour was probably due to the spirit of nitre only. Acting on this suggestion Priestley began, he tells us, 'with the solution of different metals in spirit of nitre, and catching the air, which was generated in the solution, I presently found what I wanted and a good deal more.' He had isolated the gas now known as nitric oxide, but which he called nitrous air. This paper, Sir Edward Thorpe declares, showed Priestley at his best, and he quotes at length his description of the nitric oxide and the use he made of it in measuring the goodness of air.

'One of the most conspicuous properties of this kind of air, is the great diminution of any quantity of common air with which it is mixed, attended with a turbid red, or deep orange colour, and a considerable heat. . . . The diminution of a mixture of this and common air is not an equal diminution of both the kinds, which is all that Dr. Hales could observe, but of about one-fifth of the common air, and as much of the nitrous air as is necessary to produce that effect; which, as I have found by many trials, is about one-half as much as the original quantity of common air. I hardly know any experiment that is more adapted to amaze and surprise than this is, which exhibits a quantity of air which, as it were, devours a quantity of another kind of air half

[1] Thorpe, p. 208.

H 2

as large as itself, and yet is so far from gaining any addition to its bulk that it is considerably diminished by it. . . .

'It is exceedingly remarkable that this effervescence and diminution, occasioned by the mixture of nitrous air, is peculiar to common air, or *air fit for respiration*, and, as far as I can judge from a great number of observations, is at least very nearly, if not exactly, in proportion to its fitness for this purpose; so that by this means the goodness of air may be distinguished much more accurately than it can be done by putting mice or any other animals to breathe in it.

'This was a most agreeable discovery to me, as I hope it may be a useful one to the public; especially as from this time I had no occasion for so large a stock of mice as I had been used to keep for the purpose of these experiments.' [1]

This volume also contains accounts of Priestley's discoveries of marine acid air (hydrogen chloride), and alkaline air (ammonia gas).

The second volume, published in 1775, was dedicated to Sir John Pringle. There is the usual preface with the usual gilded pill. Priestley declares that he himself hopes for no 'other kind of honour, than that of being the instrument in the hands of divine providence, which makes use of human industry to strike out, and diffuse, that knowledge of the system of nature, which seems, for some great purpose that we cannot as yet fully comprehend, to have been reserved for this age of the world; concerning which I threw out some hints in my former preface, which the excellent French translator was not permitted to insert in his version'. There is also an example of Priestley's rather simple, but nevertheless, arrogant

[1] Thorpe, p. 181–2.

habit of self-praise. 'I even think', he writes, 'that I may
flatter myself so much, if it be any flattery, as to say that
there is not, in the whole compass of philosophical
writing, a history of experiments so truly *ingenuous* as
mine, and especially the Section on the discovery of
dephlogisticated air, which I will venture to exhibit as a
model of its kind.'

Priestley has here referred to his greatest discovery of
oxygen. As far back as 1771 he had prepared oxygen
from nitre but had not realized what it was. But on
August 1st, 1774, in the laboratory at Bowood, the small
room at the end of the long library, Priestley first knew
that he had found something surprising. Apparently, so
he says, it was chance that led him on in these discoveries.
His prefatory remarks illustrate his rather haphazard
manner of working.

'The contents of this section will furnish a very
striking illustration of the truth of a remark which I
have more than once made in my philosophical
writings, and which can hardly be too often repeated,
as it tends greatly to encourage philosophical investigations; viz. that more is owing to what we call *chance*,
that is, philosophically speaking, to the observations of
events arising from unknown causes, than to any proper
design, or preconceived *theory* in this business. This
does not appear in the works of those who write *syn-
thetically* upon these subjects; but would, I doubt
not, appear very strikingly in those who are the most
celebrated for their philosophical acumen, did they
write analytically and ingenuously.

'For my own part, I will frankly acknowledge, that
at the commencement of the experiments recited in this
section, I was so far from having formed any hypothesis
that led to the discoveries I made in pursuing them,

that they would have appeared very improbable to me had I been told of them; and when the decisive facts did at length obtrude themselves upon my notice, it was very slowly, and with great hesitation, that I yielded to the evidence of my senses. And yet, when I re-consider the matter, and compare my last discoveries relating to the constitution of the atmosphere with the first, I see the closest connexion between them, so as to wonder that I should not have been led immediately from the one to the other. That this was not the case, I attribute to the force of prejudice, which, unknown to ourselves, biasses not only our *judgement*, properly so called, but even the perceptions of our senses; for we may take a maxim so strongly for granted, that the plainest evidence of sense will not entirely change, and often hardly modify, our persuasions; and the more ingenious a man is the more effectively he is entangled in his errors; his ingenuity only helping him to deceive himself, by evading the force of truth.' [1]

It had always been taken for granted that atmospherical air, like water, was an '*elemental substance,* indestructible, and unalterable'. But his experiments on air in which a candle had burnt out, and its restoration by the process of vegetation had led Priestley to question this hypothesis, though he owns he had no idea that air better than common air might be obtained. [1] Later he realized that the air he had already obtained from nitre was oxygen, but his previous discovery played no part in the latter. On August 1st he extracted oxygen, or dephlogisticated air, as he called it, from mercurius calcinatus *per se*. [2] Priestley was surprised to find that a candle burnt in it with a large

[1] Thorpe, 193.   [2] Mercuric oxide made by heating quicksilver in air.

flame, and he was utterly at a loss how to account for it. At
the same time he 'extracted a quantity of air, with the very
same property, from the common red precipitate,[1] which,
being produced by a solution of mercury in spirit of
nitre, made me conclude that this peculiar property,
being similar to that of the modification of nitrous air
above mentioned, depended on something being communicated to it by the nitrous acid'. Priestley's first
inclination was to doubt his evidence and suspect the
mercurius calcinatus of being merely red precipitate.
Being in Paris in October he procured through his
friend Magalhaens a specimen of mercurius calcinatus
from M. Cadet, of the genuineness of which there could
be no doubt.[2]

Priestley made mention of his discovery to Lavoisier,
Le Roy, and the other scientists he met.[3] This is important as showing that Lavoisier, in his subsequent
experiments on oxygen, had Priestley's hypothesis to
work on, and that he therefore had no right to claim
independent discovery. Priestley mentioned the fact of
this meeting in the original account of his discovery, and
when Lavoisier wrote in his *Elements of Chemistry* 'This
species of air was discovered almost at the same time by
Mr. Priestley, and Mr. Scheele and myself', Priestley
contradicted the assertion in the Appendix to his *Doctrine
of Phlogiston Established* and again described the dinner
party at which he had announced the discovery. But as
early as 1775 Priestley had noted Lavoisier's tendency to
plagiarism, for writing to Mr. Henry of Manchester he
said, 'He (M. Lavoisier) is an *Intendant of the Finances*,
and has much public business, but finds leisure for various
philosophical pursuits, for which he is exceedingly well

---

[1] Mercuric oxide made by heating mercuric nitrate.   [2] Thorpe, p. 195.
[3] *Air*, ii. 109.

qualified. He ought to have acknowledged that my giving him an account of the air I had got from *Mercurius Calcinatus*, and buying a quantity of M. Cadet, while I was at Paris, led him to try what air it yielded, which he did presently after I left. I have, however, barely hinted at this in my second volume.'[1] On his return from Paris Priestley proceeded to experiment with the mercurius calcinatus he had procured from M. Cadet and met with the same results he had before. But as yet he had no suspicion what kind of air he had procured. In fact he was so little aware of his discovery that if he had not at hand, as he himself relates, a lighted candle, he would never have tried it in his new air.[2] He still believed it to be common air, and even after he had experimented with a mouse and found it lived twice as long as in common air, he was surprised to find, when testing it with nitrous air, that it was better than common air. Priestley now concluded that atmospheric air consisted of nitrous acid and earth, and thus was totally blind to the meaning of his own discoveries. It was left to Lavoisier to explain and build on Priestley's facts the theory of the new chemistry.

This volume contains as well Priestley's investigations into fixed air, and Franklin was probably referring to this part when he wrote: 'I find that you have set all the philosophers of Europe to work upon *fixed air*, and it is with pleasure I observe how high you stand in their opinion; for I enjoy my friend's fame as my own.' Priestley's experiments had led him to throw out a jocular hint that he did not despair of finding the philosopher's stone, which drew the request from Franklin, that if he did, he should take care to lose it again.[3]

In the same volume is Priestley's paper on Fluor Acid

[1] William Henry, *Estimate of Philosophical Character of Dr. Priestley*, p. 15.
[2] *Air*, ii. 114.   [3] Rutt, i. 297, Jan. 27th, 1777.

Air (silicon fluoride), already discovered by Scheele the Swedish chemist, who had about the same time, and entirely independent of Priestley, discovered oxygen. Priestley always kept a childlike *naïveté* and delight in the appearance of his experiments. In this experiment he admitted the air through quicksilver into the water.

'It is then very pleasing to observe, that the moment any bubble of air, after passing through the quicksilver, reaches the water, it is instantly, as it were, converted into a stone; but continuing hollow for a short space of time, generally rises to the top of the water, in the form of a bubble, or a thin white film. If the succession of bubbles be rapid, and they rise freely to the top of the vessel, through a large body of clear water (which, however, is not always the case, as they will sometimes adhere to the upper surface of quicksilver) I have met with few persons who are soon weary of looking at it; and some could sit by it almost a whole hour, and be agreeably amused all the time.'[1]

The third volume, dedicated to Lord Stanhope, as good a Radical as was Priestley, contains two papers of importance. In one, entitled *Experiments on the Mixture of Different Kinds of Air that have no mutual action*, Priestley indicated 'the principle of the intradiffusion of gases'.[2] In another, *Respiration and the Use of Blood*, while correctly stating the processes, he quite failed to explain them.

Priestley dedicated Volume IV to Sir George Savile, one of his earliest patrons. He had, he says in his preface, promised the public a respite from his scientific publications, intending to devote more time to his metaphysical speculations, but these latter had not taken as long as he

[1] *Air*, ii. 344–6, and Thorpe, p. 199.   [2] Thorpe, p. 202.

had expected. Metaphysics were light work compared with chemistry, and single sections of his scientific work had taken him more time than whole volumes of the other —a remark which goes far to explain the impermanence of the philosophical writings. And if by chance Priestley refrains from doing some Christian propaganda among his sceptical scientists, he improves the occasion with a little moralizing. He preaches the glory of work.

> 'Man is a being endued by his creator with excellent faculties, and not to have *serious objects of pursuit* is to debase and degrade himself. It is to rank himself with beings of a lower order, aiming at nothing that is much higher than the low pleasures they are capable of; at the same time that, from the remains of noble powers, of which he cannot wholly divest himself, he is incapable of that unalloyed enjoyment of sensual pleasures that brutes have.'

In this preface Priestley attacks the danger of theorizing from facts too soon, and declares that he, for one, has always been ready to abandon conclusions should the evidence not support them. Unfortunately this statement is of only partial truth, for Priestley stuck through thick and thin, despite the contrary evidence of his own discoveries, to the theory of phlogiston.

This volume contains experiments on the antiseptic qualities of nitric oxide. By means of it Priestley tried to preserve meat and eat it six months later. But he found it was horrible, though his friend Magalhaens considered it not so bad. We can imagine Mrs. Priestley's objection to the strange invasion of her spotless kitchen.

The fifth volume contains the discovery of nitrous oxide. In the preface to the sixth there is another testimony of the relative speed of Priestley as theologian and

scientist. The six volumes which make up his Corruptions of Christianity, and the Early Opinions concerning
Christ, had taken no longer to write than one volume of
Air. No wonder the critics of the former found it easy to
point out inaccuracies! The most important experiments
in this volume are on the seeming conversion of water
into air, in which Priestley misled himself and the whole
Lunar Society, that group of Birmingham men which
met monthly at the full moon for discussion of philosophical and scientific questions. These papers threw no
light on the composition of water and were not republished in the later edition. But they were successful in
drawing the attention of James Watt to the subject, who
shortly afterwards, and about the same time as Cavendish,
discovered the true composition of water.

Most of Priestley's important experiments were made
at Calne. After he settled at Birmingham he spent much
time at them, and his expenses were generously defrayed
by his wealthy friends. Soon after his arrival Wedgwood
and Boulton had set to work to raise £100 per annum.
No one was to give more than 10 guineas, as a larger
subscription from any one individual would not be
respectable; but the kind-hearted and generous Wedgwood intended to evade this difficulty by putting up extra
ten guineas in the names of friends. Boulton would have
preferred that a dozen gentlemen should each subscribe
£100 wherewith they could buy the doctor an annuity,
for he thought this would be less embarrassing to his
feelings than the annual subscription. The Congregation
of the New Meeting engaged an assistant, so that Priestley
could give as much time as he liked to his experiments.

But Priestley was so intent on defending the theory of
phlogiston, which the French chemists, in particular
Lavoisier, were overthrowing by means of what he had

already found, that he had no time for fresh discoveries. Sir Edward Thorpe has drawn the attention of his readers to the extraordinary difference between Priestley as scientist and theologian.[1] In the latter capacity he is radical to the extreme, nor was his mind ever closed to new ideas. But in science all was different. Despite the adverse evidence of his own discoveries he still clung to the false hypothesis, and wasted time and energy in its defence. His last scientific paper, entitled *The Doctrine of Phlogiston Established,* was written at Northumberland, just about the time that the doctrine was finally overthrown. However sure he might be that it would prevail he realized that at that moment he was alone against the world. 'In this country', he declared, 'I have not heard of a single advocate for phlogiston. In England they are very few, and none of them have written anything on the subject. In France they are still fewer.'[2]

But for all Priestley's failures to theorize correctly, he still remains one of the great chemists of the modern world. He looked on science like all pursuit of truth, as leading to the greater glory of God, and he never attempted to add to his own glory by keeping anything secret. His friends, especially his companions in the Lunar Society, were kept well in touch with whatever was going on in his laboratory, and he exchanged ideas with any or all of them, long before the completion of any experiment. He has likened the experimenter to the hound worrying in the covert for whatever he could find, and this description is at least true of himself. His habit of rushing rapidly from one work to the next is probably the reason why so much of his work was superficial. It is related of Priestley's eccentric brother-in-law, John Wilkinson, that when he had some great idea he wished to think out, he would

[1] Cf. Thorpe, p. 168.   [2] *Doctrine of Phlogiston,* Preface.

stay in bed and ponder over it, with a heavy leaden ball in his hand which, should he become sleepy, would fall and wake him up.[1] Priestley might have done better had he followed Wilkinson's example and given more time to thought. As it was, moving backwards and forwards from his chemistry to his theology, metaphysics, and pastoral work, he can have given himself little time to consider facts and bring forth conclusions. Added to this, Priestley suffered from a very bad memory. In his auto-biography he recounts how twice he did exactly the same piece of work without having any idea of it, and how he was horrified at finding the first piece of writing. After-wards he invented some kind of mechanical device to avoid such mistakes, but no mechanical device could be a real substitute. Had he had a better memory, it is possible that he would have seen his own discoveries, and those of others, in their mutual bearing, and might have abandoned his favourite theory of phlogiston.

[1] Randall, *The Wilkinsons.*

CHAPTER VIII
METAPHYSICS

METAPHYSICS, as that branch of speculative inquiry which treats of the first principles of things, was certain in the days when science was by no means the specialized study it has now become, to attract a thinker like Priestley, himself a dabbler—sometimes more than a dabbler—in many things, and a theologian at heart.

Priestley was well advanced in middle life before he published his metaphysical books, but the subject was not new to him. At school he had read Locke, and at the Academy had studied 'Pneumatology', as psychology was then called. But of all the books he read it was the study of Hartley's *Observations on Man* that left the deepest impression on him.

David Hartley, a man of mild and lovable character, lived during the first half of the eighteenth century. Originally he intended taking orders, but some scruples prevented his signing the articles, and instead he became a physician. In 1749 appeared his *Observations on Man*, the outcome of sixteen years of thought and study. This work is of lasting importance in the history of psychology, for in it Hartley attempted to explain all mental phenomena on physical grounds, and if the form of the hypothesis is wrong, the hypothesis itself is right 'that mind and body always co-operate and there is a physical equivalent for the mental, and a mental equivalent for the physical, operation in every case'.[1] Thus Hartley should be regarded as the father of physiological psychology.

Hartley's particular hypothesis was his doctrine of vibrations, taken and developed to some extent from Sir Isaac Newton. He supposed that the ether was diffused

[1] Brett, *History of Psychology*, ii. 279.

through the pores of bodies as well as through all space. External objects set going vibrations in the ether, which were communicated to the pores of the nerves, which set vibrating, in pendulum-like motion, the particles of the nerves until the vibrations were extended to the brain. Thus sensations and their dependent ideas were conveyed from the outside object to the brain. Their connexion and relation to each other, as likewise all the faculties of the mind, Hartley explained by his theory of the Association of Ideas. The theory did not originate with Hartley, but he was the first writer to try to explain all mental phenomena thus. During the eighteenth century his book was very little read. Apparently he did not expect it to be. Priestley republished his *Observations* in 1775,[1] omitting the doctrine of vibrations, and theological essays, not because he was in disagreement, but because he believed the theory of the Association of Ideas was more likely to be accepted without them. Priestley made very little original contribution to the metaphysics and psychology of the century, but in accepting Hartley so whole-heartedly he showed himself to be years before his generation. It was not until the nineteenth century that James Mill made Hartley the foundation of his school of Association Psychology.

In spite of his materialist explanation of mental phenomena, Hartley still believed in an immaterial principle and even held that there might be 'an intermediate elementary body between the mind and the gross body'.[2] This was quite unnecessary as his theories explained man without its need, and it was rejected by his more logical followers. As early as 1768 Priestley had declared that his faith in the resurrection depended on revealed, not

---

[1] In 1782 Priestley's *Hartley* was burnt 'by the licensers at Brussels'. Rutt, i. 341.   [2] Priestley's *Hartley*.

natural religion, and had horrified the eccentric Thomas
Amory by asserting, in the course of conversation, that
if his idea of immortality rested on nature, 'I should never
think of a remove from the clods of the valley'.[1] In his
first Essay prefatory to Hartley, he drops the suggestion
almost casually that he is 'inclined to think' that man does
not consist of two things so entirely different as matter
and spirit.

Until he produced his *Disquisitions* Priestley had
scarcely entered the metaphysical arena. It is true that
he had attacked the 'Scotch Doctors', Reid, Beatty, and
Oswald, for their attempt to oppose the scepticism of
Hume by an appeal to common sense and by the cham-
pioning of innate ideas, which Priestley believed to
have been finally overthrown by Locke and his beloved
Hartley. As a controversialist, Priestley is not enjoyable.
He is bad tempered and superior, his ridicule heavy, and
the reader tires of his frequent phrase, 'I flatter myself'.

It was during the dark days of the American Revolution
that Priestley set out to declare what were his notions as
to ultimate reality. So unpopular was the work that its
publication was supposed to have injured Lord Shelburne
with the public, and the efforts of all his friends, 'true
friends,'[2] said Horne Tooke, were unavailing to stop its
publication. Benjamin Vaughan accused Priestley of obstinacy.[3] One suspects that the more Shelburne's friends
tried to stop the publication, the more Priestley felt it
his duty not to be silent in the cause of truth.

The *Disquisitions relating to Matter and Spirit* were
published in 1777 and were aimed against the Arian
hypothesis of the pre-existence[4] of the soul. Priestley
does not build up his theories on a solid bed-rock of fact,

---

[1] John Buncle, *Theological Repository*, ii.   [2] Horne Tooke Notes.
[3] *Belloc-Lowndes MSS.*   [4] *Disquisitions,* i., Dedication.

but mistakes his theories for fact. Thus behind his reasoning are the two preconceived ideas that 'God is' and that 'He is good'. From these it may be deduced that his purposes towards man will be beneficent and that therefore the end of man will be unlimited happiness. To understand Priestley's writings it is necessary to keep this in mind.

Priestley begins his work with the laudable and very modern intention of giving his hypothesis a scientific basis. Before he explains man he gives his theory of matter, derived largely from Boscovich, and already referred to in his *Vision, Light, and Colours*. Matter is composed of minute particles called atoms at that time, but molecules in modern scientific language. Their essential qualities are powers of attraction and repulsion, and, according to Boscovich, 'the atom itself, has no parts or dimension. In its geometrical aspect it is a mere geometrical point. It has no extension in space. It has not the so-called property of Impenetrability, for two atoms may exist in the same place.'[1] Priestley seized hold with delight of this idea of the penetrability of matter. The objection to the materiality of man, he supposed, was found in the popular idea of matter 'as *solid* and *inert*, being incapable of the powers of sensation and thought'.[2] He sees that man is neither immaterial spirit or dead matter, but it is not as a living organism, but as a machine that Priestley explains him.

Powers of attraction and repulsion, the essential qualities of matter, are easily accounted for as instances of the divine power, but they are not the Deity Himself.[3] Priestley is anxious to make sure, perhaps wisely for the age in which he lived, if less so for his future fame as a

---

[1] *Encyclopaedia Britannica*, 'Molecules'.   [2] *Disquisitions*, i. 33.
[3] Ibid. i. 41.

I

philosopher, that his theory had nothing whatever to do with that of Spinoza,[1] whom he had probably never read, except in translations and abridgements.

From his theory of matter Priestley proceeds to explain that the sentient principle in man, by which he means the soul, exists in the brain. 'The powers of sensation and thought, as belonging to man', he says, 'have never been found but in conjunction with a certain *organized system of matter*.'[2] 'There is no instance of any man retaining the faculty of thinking when the brain is destroyed.'[3] He noted the close connexion between mind and body, and their mutual reaction. From the fact that parts of the mind may be destroyed before death, he argues that the mind will be totally extinguished at death.[4]

One of the strong points of his system, he urges, is that it does away with many difficulties. No longer need we wonder what happens to the soul in sleep, or swooning, or when the body is apparently dead as in drowning;[5] nor are we faced with such questions as to the time of entry of the soul into the embryo; and if it is a new created spirit, or some pre-existent one which has been waiting since all eternity for this moment to descend to earth.[6]

Then there is the similarity of animals with man, for they differ from each other in degree, not in kind. If the soul of man is something different from his body, must animals, too, have some immaterial principle?[7]

Priestley was quite right when he pointed out that the vulgar, who believe in spirits, look on them as 'a kind of attenuated aerial substance',[8] and that the only idea of God they have is of Him as some material being. He held that since they were such disparate substances, it was impossible for soul and body to have any connexion at

---

[1] *Disquisitions* i. 42.   [2] Ibid. i. 46.   [3] Ibid. i. 47.   [4] Ibid. i. 48, 49.
[5] Ibid. i. 61.   [6] Ibid. i. 61, 62.   [7] Ibid. i. 62.   [8] Ibid. i. 72.

all with each other. 'This', says Priestley, is 'a difficulty and a mystery that we cannot comprehend',[1] like the doctrines of Transubstantiation and the Trinity. Mystery is often but another word for ignorance. Of course this trouble, like so many more, was easily enough met with the explanation of the Will of God. But, may we not ask, does not the same difficulty exist with an immaterial God at work on a material universe?

The difficulty of explaining thought exists whether we adopt a material or immaterial hypothesis, 'for, in fact, we have no distinct idea either of the *properties*, or of the *substance* of mind or spirit'.[2] If we argue ourselves into believing that the subject of thought is 'simple, indivisible, immaterial, or unnaturally immortal'[3] by fancying 'that it is something we feel, or are conscious of'[4] it is more than likely we deceive our own selves.

Priestley realizes that the great objection to his system is that, as the mind is but part of the body, it too will be liable to corruption, though immateriality does not necessarily imply immortality:[5] but if the immaterialists have had recourse to the Deity to make their system work, Priestley can build a separate system of immortality on the strength of revealed religion.

Having explained his universe and man on a materialist basis, one wonders how Priestley will deal with God, who is necessary to him as the author of revealed religion, on whose promise he builds all his hope of resurrection. He very wisely begins by remarking that the Deity is a subject beyond all human comprehension and that this fact has given rise to diverse opinions.[6] Hence we should learn diffidence in asserting our own and charity in judging other people's.

---

[1] Ibid. i. 80. [2] Ibid. i. 112. [3] Ibid. i. 134. [4] Ibid. i. 134.
[5] Ibid. i. 130. [6] Ibid. i. 138.

One may imagine Priestley's orthodox readers approaching this chapter with all the excitement of a pack of hounds nearing upon its quarry. If only the Heretic should prove his God to be the same as the material universe he can be confined in Hell with the atheist Hobbes and the impious Spinoza. Priestley is aware of the dangers that surround him, but he is not affrighted. He is prepared to deal with all difficulties, whether propounded by himself or others.[1] He declares we know nothing of matter apart from its powers.[2] Take away its powers and we have no idea of it left. How then can we suppose we know anything of the Divine Being apart from His powers, properties, and attributes? Perhaps the modern reader is not quite so sure as is our author of these powers, properties, and attributes. Priestley declares that the attributes of God, such as omniscience and omnipotence, are so different from anything that we find in man that we cannot argue the materiality of God from analogy.[3] 'All that we can pretend to know of God is his infinite wisdom, power, and goodness.'[4] We suppose His existence as there must be some first cause, 'but of the nature of the *existence* of this primary cause, concerning which we know nothing but by its *effects*, we cannot have any conception. We are absolutely confounded, bewildered, and lost, when we attempt to speculate concerning it.'[5] To the possible accusation that he may make the Deity a material being, Priestley replies that he has no idea of the divine essence at all different from those philosophers who maintain the proper omnipresence and ubiquity of the Divine Being, 'which necessarily implies a real extension, and that he has power of acting upon matter.'[6]

---

[1] *Disquisitions*, i. 139. [2] Ibid. i. 140. [3] Ibid. i. 142.
[4] Ibid. i. 144. [5] Ibid. i. 146. [6] Ibid. i. 149.

He asserts that his opinion of the materiality of man has nothing whatsoever to do with the idea of God, but since materialism is supposed to lead to Atheism, he is willing to show that our practical knowledge of God stands independent of any conception whatever concerning even the divine essence' [1] let alone any doctrine of human nature. By God is meant an intelligent first cause.[2] Priestley deduces this from the belief that the world must have had a maker and a design since the parts fit in so well together.

Immortality conceived of as the resurrection of the body is a more difficult belief to hold or argue for, than when it is considered as spiritual. But Priestley would be no Christian were he not to champion immortality, and as he allows of no spirit, the resurrection must be of the body. Identity of a man he supposes to be continuity of consciousness, and he does not consider the composition of the physical body important. Priestley allows that if at the resurrection 'we shall know one another again, and converse together as before, we shall be, to all intents and purposes, *the same persons*'.[3] But for himself Priestley believed the resurrection of the body in a stricter sense. Death is a decomposition, and 'whatever is decomposed may be recomposed by the Being who first composed it'.[4] This resurrection will not be miraculous, but will be according to some unknown law of Nature.[5]

In Sections 14, 15, and 16, Priestley attempted to prove his theories by biblical quotations, always a dangerous method, and to later thought quite unsatisfactory. But in the latter part of the *Disquisitions*, in the 'History of the Philosophic Doctrine concerning the Origin of the Soul', and the 'Nature of Matter', he is quite in sympathy with

[1] Ibid. i. 186. [2] Ibid. i. 186. [3] Ibid. i. 199.
[4] Ibid. i. 200. [5] Ibid. i. 202.

the ideas of modern scholarship. His knowledge may be inadequate and faulty at times, but here, as in his later theological works, his object is to account for and understand doctrines in their historical setting. If he did not succeed in making a permanent contribution to knowledge, he at least pointed the way in which others should follow.

Priestley, as a schoolboy, had been a firm believer in the freedom of the will, and had carried on, before his Daventry days, a correspondence in its defence with Peter Annet, a deistic writer. Unfortunately for his own sake, Annet was converted neither to Priestley's philosophical nor theological opinions, for at the age of 70 in 1763 he was sentenced to a year's imprisonment and to stand twice in the pillory for having, in his *Free Inquirer*, ridiculed the Old Testament.[1]

It was the perusal of Anthony Collins' *Human Liberty* that converted Priestley to belief in Philosophic Necessity, a belief strengthened by the study of Hartley's *Observations on Man*. From his theory of the Association of Ideas, the latter had deduced that the mind of man was mechanistic, and as much subject to the laws of cause and effect as any other parts of nature. In fact, Hartley was one of those with whom cause was 'a hallowed altar, on which we were summoned to make a burnt-offering of human freedom'.[2] Hartley, devout man, inspired by love to God, was sure that a benevolent being had at heart the ultimate, unlimited happiness of the human race. Though evil existed, and unmerited suffering, yet there was more happiness than misery in the world. The pious mind could find in 'all partial evil, universal good', and would come to discover happiness, even in its own suffering.

[1] *D.N.B.*   [2] Knox, *Will to be Free*, p. 109.

Much of the freewill controversy as dealt with by Priestley and his opponents was theological in origin and enhanced by the ambiguity of terms. In psychology, freedom of the will means the ability to decide or choose for oneself, but in metaphysics, that will or decisions have no cause. Thus freedom in the first sense is usually admitted, and Priestley grants it all when he says, 'I would observe, that I allow to man all the liberty, or power, that is *possible in itself*, and to which the ideas of mankind in general ever go, which is the *power of doing whatever they will or please.*' [1]

He considers that the will should not be regarded as a separate faculty, but as the mind when it wills or desires, and as governed just as is the mind in any other capacities by the Association of Ideas. Hartley and Priestley are both hedonists in as much as they suppose that the mind desires some particular object because it will give it pleasure. But they both undermine their hedonism by admitting qualitative pleasures. Hartley considered that 'the pure love of God' was our highest and ultimate perfection, 'our end, centre, and only resting-place,' [2] a remark extremely reminiscent of Spinoza's intellectual love of God. Priestley rightly considered man's highest delight to be in acting in conformity with the divine will. In fact, viewed aright, everything must be in accordance with the divine will, and this alone would eliminate any possibility of a self-determining will in man, for there is but 'one will in the whole universe' and 'this one will, exclusive of all chance, or the interference of any other will, disposes of all things, even to their minutest circumstances, and always for the best of purposes'. [3]

Priestley's philosophic necessity is very much the

[1] *Disquisitions*, ii. 2.　　[2] Hartley, i. 497.　　[3] *Disquisitions*, ii., p. xi.

handmaid of his theology. His necessarian regards himself as the instrument of the Almighty, 'though at the same time, as the object', and considers temper, will, and conduct as His gifts, for which he will humbly pray.[1] In such an organized universe, rewards and punishments have their proper place as incentives for better actions, and should not be regarded as the results.

If man is but the instrument of God, and if in the long chain of cause and effect, no event can be different, can he be held responsible to God for his conduct? One of the strongest objections urged against necessity is that it does away with man's accountability. How, it is said, can the potter blame his vessels if they are bad? This difficulty was increased in theology by the contradictory notions of God as creator and judge. Priestley, as moralist and theologian, perforce must defend man's accountability. He is perfectly right in supposing that a man's own state of mind and his character are as much causes determining the will as are external facts. But when he asserts that a man's own actions and determination are necessary links in the long chain of cause and effect, and that a man's success or failure depend upon himself,[2] he is inconsistent. For, in the first case, man must be determined, and the second, if it means anything, must mean that Priestley is allowing man initiative. 'That we ourselves may be the authors of genuine novelty is the doctrine of free will.'[3] A few pages back we left our pious necessarian praying for a right 'temper, will and conduct' as God's gifts, and it is scarcely fair that Priestley should turn on him because the Almighty has not listened to his prayer.

Even if we may suppose that Priestley has doubts as to his own consistency, his philosopher is protected from

[1] *Disquisitions*, ii. 80.   [2] Ibid. ii. 108.
[3] William James, *Some Problems of Philosophy*, p. 145.

any harmful results that might follow by the statement
that in ordinary every day life he will steer his course by
the same stars as his fellow men.[1] In fact, one might say
the 'illusion' of freedom is of more use in this world than
the 'truth, of necessity. 'Then damn his philosophy',
noted Horne Tooke, 'for it is not worth a carrot'; and
adds, when Priestley declares he is considering his
philosopher retired from the world, 'Hang him at once,
for he has no business in the world.' [2]

But Priestley is not really considering the philosopher
at all, but his idea of a Christian; and he was but asserting
his own faith when he wrote:

'The connexion that all persons, and all things necessarily have, as parts of an immense, glorious, and happy
system (and of which we ourselves are part, however
small and inconsiderable) with the great author of this
system, makes us regard every person, and every thing,
in a friendly and pleasing light. The whole is but *one
family*. We have all *one God and Father*, whose affection
for us is intense, impartial, and everlasting. He *despises
nothing that he has made*, and by ways unknown
to us, and often by methods most unpromising, he
provides for our greatest good. We are all training
up in the same school of moral discipline, and are
likewise *joint heirs of eternal life*, revealed to us in the
gospel.' [3]

Priestley does not shrink from the conclusion that if
God be the cause of all things, then He must be the cause
of evil. Calvinist necessarians, like Jonathan Edwards
and Augustus Toplady, Priestley's correspondent, remembered as the author of *Rock of Ages*, had met this

---

[1] *Disquisitions*, ii. 118.   [2] Horne Tooke Notes.
[3] *Disquisitions*, ii. 123.

difficulty with the quibble that God did not cause, but merely permitted evil. Priestley allows God to be the cause, but avoids the inference that in that case the Deity can be no perfect being, by contending that it is the motives which are good or bad, not actions.[1] Thus God, like the proverbial Jesuit, may inflict evil that good may come of it, conduct which would be wrong in any but an omniscient being, as he alone can be sure of the desired result.[2] Evil, on the assumption that the universe is perfect, is hard to account for, and somehow the solution that Priestley supported, that pain and anguish were divine discipline, is unsatisfying. Misfortune does not distinguish between the deserving and undeserving, the good and bad. Priestley might dread French philosophy, but there is more humanity in the ridicule of Voltaire than in the 'Whatever is, is right' of Pope or Hartley.

But it should be remembered that when he, too, was overcome with misfortune, Priestley stood by his necessarian principles, and believed that in the end everything would work out for the best, even did he occasionaly allow himself to bear rancour against the instruments of the Deity, in the shape of his enemies.

Necessity must not be confused with Calvinist predestination. To Priestley the idea of the divine goodness was incompatible with the doctrine of Hell. God's glory, man's damnation was false to him, and here his scheme of necessity parted company from that of Edwards and Toplady. The former believed that the number of the elect would be small, and that their joy in heaven would be greatly increased by watching the torments of the damned. Toplady, on the other hand, thought that the majority, inclusive of all 'young persons', would be saved, though he was angry with Priestley for attributing to him

[1] *Disquisitions*, ii. 131.   [2] Ibid. ii. 133.

the charitable, if unscriptural, belief that the pains of Hell would not last for ever and ever. Toplady disputed Priestley's assertion that necessity was more compatible with Socinianism than Calvinism. 'Seriously', he wrote to Priestley, 'I think you have admitted a Trojan horse into your gates, whose concealed force will probably, at the long run, display the banner of John Calvin on your walls, and master your capital, though at present garrisoned by the confederate forces of Pelagius, Sozzo, and Van Harnim.'[1] However little scriptural justification Priestley had for sharing Hartley's opinion that 'ultimate unlimited happiness' was the end of all things, he did at least conceive of God, not as a cruel and implacable tyrant, inferior to man in sympathy, pity and justice, but as a gracious and loving Father.

The attacks which followed the publication of these two books were mostly inspired by theology. Priestley's materialism was held up to much ridicule, and he and Berkeley between them were supposed to have annihilated man. 'Bishop Berkeley tells me', wrote Toplady in a friendly letter, 'that I am all spirit, without a single particle of matter belonging to me. Dr. Priestley, on the other hand, contends that I am all body, untenanted and unanimated by any immaterial substance within. Put these two theories together, and what will be the product? That my sum total, and that of every other man, amounts to just nothing at all. I have neither body nor soul; I have no sort of existence whatever.'[2]

Priestley's attack on spirit was thought to have endangered belief in immortality, and there must be many, who, in opposition to him, hold that if all hope of immortality depends on the resurrection of revealed religion, they would build little hope thereon. Perhaps Horne

[1] Rutt, i. 260.   [2] Ibid. i. 310.

Tooke was wise in wanting two strings to his bow, the authorities of natural and revealed religion.

Not all the criticisms were serious:

> Here lies at rest,
> In oaken chest,
> Together packed most nicely,
> The bones and brains,
> Flesh, blood and veins,
> And soul of Dr. Priestley. [1]

sang the Welsh poet David Davis. And when Dr. Price repeated this epitaph to him, Priestley was delighted with it.

To the popular mind, materialism was synonymous with atheism. It must be conceded that there is some justification for this view of Priestley's materialism. His religion was built on the sandy foundation of revealed religion, a foundation that was to be undermined by science, and the Higher Criticism, of which Priestley was a forerunner. Nowadays it would probably be impossible to find any one who, holding ideas of materialism, also held to the belief in revealed religion.

[1] *Monthly Repository*, i, New Series, 694–5.

CHAPTER IX

BIRMINGHAM

1780–91

IN his *History of the Rebellion* Clarendon declared that Birmingham, or Bromicham, as he preferred to call it, was 'of as great fame for hearty, wilful, affected disloyalty to the king, as any place in England'.[1] Naturally, in such soil, Presbyterianism took root, and though with the advent of the House of Hanover disloyalty disappeared, Birmingham has ever since numbered Nonconformists among her most illustrious sons.

When Priestley came to Birmingham in 1780 it had long been an important centre of manufactures. The recent improvement in processes had given rise to unprecedented prosperity. In advertising his history of the town, William Hutton wrote, 'her Name is echoed through the Commercial World; there is not a village without her Manufactures. This Seat of Invention furnishes Ornament and Use. Her astonishing Increase is beyond Example. The Traveller who visits her once in six Months, supposes himself well acquainted with her; but he may chance to find a Street of Houses in the Autumn, where he saw his horse at Grass in the Spring. A pitiful Market Town, in an Inland County, by pure Industry, in a few Years, surpasses most of our Cities.'[2]

The names which are most associated with Birmingham during the second half of the eighteenth century are those of Boulton and Watt. Matthew Boulton, son of another Matthew Boulton, had joined his father in business as a mere boy. He had introduced many improvements into the manufacture of buttons, watch chains, and the like.

---

[1] Clarendon, *Rebellion*, Book VII, 1843 ed., 382.
[2] Langford, i. 297.

He invented a steel buckle which became fashionable, and which was exported to France and thence introduced into England as the latest French production. Boulton's industry was indefatigable and his foresight and courage were rewarded. In 1775 he entered into partnership with James Watt for the manufacture of his steam engine. Watt had patented his engine in 1769, but it was only now that it was manufactured successfully. Connected with these two was John Wilkinson, Priestley's brother-in-law. He cast for them the 18-inch cylinder which enabled Watt's engine to run smoothly, and the first engine made by them was to his order. While his contemporaries believed it to be an idle dream, Wilkinson knew that the age of iron had arrived. At his instigation was built the first iron bridge at Coalbrookdale. He built iron barges, which to every one else's surprise, floated, to carry his goods down to the sea. The first was tried in July 1787. 'Yesterday week my iron boat was launched', wrote Wilkinson, 'answers all my expectations, and has convinced the unbelievers, who were 999 in 1,000. It will be only a nine-days' wonder, and afterwards a Columbus's egg.' [1]

Boulton and Watt were a fine example of what partners should be. Close personal friends with firm faith in each other, yet they were of entirely different characters. Boulton was courageous, cheerful and genial, fond of young and old, of quiet Quakers and noisy children. Watt, on the other hand, was shy, timid, and apprehensive. His great inventive work, like most original work, was done only at the cost of himself. He had to invent, and he had to spend himself in inventing. Headaches and weariness of the flesh resulted. The cruel attempts of others to steal his plans and upset his patents were hard

[1] Smiles, p. 213 n.

blows to such a sensitive soul. There were many occasions when he stood in need of his partner's sympathy and courage, without which his brilliant ideas might never have been successfully accomplished.

The great works at Soho were one of the principal sights of England. Hither came English lords and foreign princes. Shelburne paid a visit with his first countess. At another time Boulton was honoured by a visit from the Tsarina Catherine. 'The Empress of Russia', he wrote, 'is now at my house, and a charming woman she is.' [1] A pleasanter guest, we may suppose, than monarch. After her visit she sent Boulton her portrait. Like Wedgwood, Boulton had to suspect that each visitor of less exalted position might be a spy, ready to run off with their ideas, whether or not patented.

Priestley at once joined the Lunar Society. It had been founded by Boulton and met in turn at the houses of its members, when dinner was followed by discussion of whatsoever was uppermost in their minds. The Society was never a very formal affair. It was in existence as early as 1768, when Boulton summoned its members to meet Watt, passing that way on his journey from London to Glasgow, at 'l'hotel de l'amitié sur Handsworth Heath', for so Boulton called his house.

The Society included among its members all the most interesting men of the neighbourhood, and indeed the Lunar Society may have rivalled for interest and intelligence any other that has ever existed. Most prominent among its members for wit and ability was Erasmus Darwin, grandfather on the one side, as Josiah Wedgwood was on the other, of Charles Darwin. By profession a doctor, Darwin had built up a large practice. Had he moved to London, it is said that the Royal family would

[1] Ibid. p. 216.

have patronized him. He was a large man, and in later life corpulent and lame as the result of an accident in a carriage he had designed himself. He had a bad stammer, but whatever he said, whether seriously or in jest, was worth waiting for.[1] He was a great apostle of temperance. Interested in mechanics, he planned a windmill to grind flints for Josiah Wedgwood. He invented some kind of talking machine which led to the following agreement between him and Boulton:

'I promise to pay to Dr. Darwin of Lichfield one thousand pounds upon his delivering to me (within 2 years from date hereof) an Instrument called an organ that is capable of pronouncing the Lord's Prayer, the Creed, and Ten Commandments in the Vulgar Tongue, and his ceding to me, and me only, the property of the said invention with all the advantages thereunto appertaining.

M. BOULTON.
Soho Sept. 3rd. 17—' [2]

As an evolutionist Darwin anticipated his grandson. In both the *Botanic Garden* and the *Zoonomia* he inferred the origin of species from some common ancestor. His doctrine was similar to that of Lamarck, and differed from the younger Darwin's in considering conscious adaptation, rather than natural selection, as the means of variation.

Darwin was not a regular attendant at the meetings of the Lunar Society, for his profession often interfered with his pleasures.

'I am sorry', he wrote to Boulton, 'the infernal divinities who visit mankind with diseases, and are therefore

---

[1] Seward, *Memoirs of the Life of Dr. Darwin.*
[2] Charles Darwin, *Erasmus Darwin,* p. 121.

at perpetual war with Doctors, should have prevented my seeing all you great men at Soho to-day. Lord! what inventions, what wit, what rhetoric, metaphysical, mechanical and pyrotechnical, will be on the wing, bandied like a shuttlecock from one to another of your troop of philosophers! while poor I, I by myself, I, imprisoned in a post-chaise, am joggled, and jostled, and bump'd, and bruised along the King's high road, to make war upon a stomach-ache or a fever!' [1]

Shortly before Darwin's removal from Lichfield to Derby, and his consequent resignation from the Lunar Society, Watt wrote to him:

'I beg that you would impress on your memory the idea that you promised to dine with sundry men of learning at my house on Monday next, and that you will realize the idea. For your encouragement there is a new book to cut up, and it is to be determined whether or not heat is a compound of phlogiston and empyreal air, and whether a mirror can reflect the heat of the fire. I give you a friendly warning that you may be found wanting whichever opinion you may adopt in the latter question; therefore be cautious. If you are meek and humble, perhaps you may be told what light is made of, and also how to make it, and the theory proved by synthesis and analysis.' [2]

But Darwin could not keep this appointment.

'You know,' runs his answer, 'there is a perpetual war between the devil and all holy men. Sometimes one prevails in an odd skirmish or so, and sometimes the other. Now, you must know that this said devil has played me a slippery trick, and, I fear, prevented me from coming to join the holy men at your house,

---

[1] Smiles, p. 369.   [2] *Scientific Correspondence*, p. 201.

by sending the measles with peripneumony amongst nine beautiful children of Lord Paget's. For I must suppose it is the work of the devil! Surely the Lord could never think of amusing himself by setting nine innocent little animals to cough their hearts up. Pray, ask your learned Society if this partial evil contributes to any public good, if this pain is necessary to establish the subordination or different links in the chain of animation. If one was to be weaker and less perfect than another, must he therefore have pain as part of his portion? Pray inquire of your philosophers, and rescue me from Manichaeism.' [1]

But natural philosophy, not religion, was the subject of discussion, and we do not know if Darwin's heresy was ever answered.

Samuel Galton was another member of the Society. He was a Quaker, living at Barr. Galton's daughter, Mary Ann, afterwards Mrs. Schimmelpenninck, has left some amusing, if by no means always accurate, descriptions of the Lunar Society and its members. She held Dr. Darwin in strong disapproval, and regretted Priestley's lack of orthodoxy.

At one time Richard Lovell Edgeworth was a member. He had been settled at Lichfield, where he had married first Honora, and then Elizabeth Sneyd. Edgeworth was interested in mechanics and education. He tried to educate his eldest son on Rousseau-like principles, and the chief characteristic of the boy was unruliness. On a visit to Paris, Edgeworth took his son to see Rousseau, and asked the philosopher for his opinion. Rousseau took young Richard for a walk. On his return he told the father that he thought him a boy of abilities, 'But,' said Rousseau, 'I

[1] *Scientific Correspondence*, p. 202.

remark in your son a propensity to party prejudice, which will be a great blemish.' For whenever the boy had seen a handsome horse or carriage, he had exclaimed, 'That is an English horse, or an English carriage!' And that, even down to a pair of shoe buckles, everything that appeared to be good of its kind was always pronounced by him to be English.'[1] Edgeworth's friend Thomas Day, author of *Sandford and Merton*, was at some period another member of the Lunar Society.

Contemporaneous with Priestley's membership was that of James Keir. Keir had been born an eighteenth child, at Edinburgh, where he had attended the University at the same time as Darwin. Later he joined the Army and was sent to the West Indies. On retiring from the active list he settled first at Stourbridge and later at Birmingham. 'He was the wit, the man of the world, the finished gentleman, who gave life and animation to the party.'[2] William Withering, the botanist, was another leading light of the Society.

When Priestley severed his connexion with Lord Shelburne he did not immediately look out for a new position. His annuity of £150 was a larger income than he had enjoyed at Leeds. But he thought Calne expensive, and probably the nearness to his late patron was now an embarrassment. He had friends in Birmingham already, and its scientific society was an attraction. Besides, his brother-in-law, John Wilkinson, desired him to settle near at hand. Wilkinson himself cannot have been altogether a sympathetic character, but his wealth and position were such that they might be relied on to give Priestley's growing sons the best possible start in life. Mrs. Priestley was of an affectionate nature, and fond of both brothers, who were usually on bad terms. After one

---

[1] Edgeworth, *Memoirs*, i. 255.   [2] Schimmelpenninck, i. 36.

quarrel, William migrated to France, where he taught the French to cast cannon.[1]

Priestley left Calne at Michaelmas, 1780. It is to be hoped that Mrs. Priestley did not again allow her husband to superintend the fastening of the boxes, for, on the occasion of their removal from Leeds he had undertaken the supervision; on unpacking, Mrs. Priestley found he had put under the cover of each box mineralogical specimens, and a number of chemical mixtures. 'The doctor begged her not to distress herself if the clothes were a little injured, for the minerals had come perfectly well.'[2]

The Priestleys settled at Fairhill, which, in those days, was a little distance out of Birmingham. When Faujas de Saint-Fond visited it he declared it 'a charming house, with a fine meadow on the one side and a delightful garden on the other. There was an air of the most perfect neatness in every thing connected with this house, both without and within it. I know not how to give a better idea of it than by comparing it to those snug houses so often to be met with in Holland, particularly on the road from Harlem [*sic*] to Leyden, and from Leyden to the Hague.'[3] Here Priestley brought his collection of philosophical instruments, which, during the next ten years, was to grow into one of the best in the world. Here, too, he had his library 'rendered valuable by a choice of excellent works'.

Shortly after his removal to Birmingham, Priestley was asked by the congregation of the New Meeting to become its minister. It had the reputation of being the most liberal congregation in England. The pastoral duties were not heavy, as Priestley had the assistance of

[1] Young, *Travels*, p. 134.   [2] Schimmelpenninck, i. 85–6.
[3] Faujas de Saint-Fond, ii. 342

Mr. Blyth, the colleague of his predecessor; but though he was relieved of a great part of the ordinary duties, he still had the Sunday services, and the religious instruction of the children of the congregation. He says he greatly improved his plan of catechizing and lecturing, and introduced the custom of expounding the scriptures as he read them, which he had never done before.

In the years before the French Revolution, Priestley's most important work lay in the field of controversial divinity. The *Theological Repository* was revived and another three volumes published. The neighbouring Dissenting ministers met him fortnightly, when they read and selected papers for the *Repository*. But this periodical did not flourish and eventually had to be given up. In 1782 Priestley published his *History of the Corruptions of Christianity*. He had originally intended to make it the fourth volume of his *Institutes of Natural and Revealed Religion*, but the work had expanded until it was larger than the whole of the *Institutes*. That work had been avowedly popular, and Priestley had made no attempt to go to original writers, contenting himself with such authorities as Le Clerc and Mosheim. When the *History of the Corruptions of Christianity* grew and became a work for 'a higher class of readers', he felt it important to go beyond, and therefore, as he said, had 'taken a good deal of pains to read, or at least look carefully through, many of the most capital works of the Christian writers'.[1] At the same time he claimed to be using the historical method. He aimed at tracing each corruption to its proper source, but he scandalizes the modern historian, for he had made up his mind already as to what were the corruptions. He did not read his authorities and then come to conclusions; he first of all arrived at his conclusions and then

[1] *Corruptions of Christianity*, Preface.

read his authorities for support. For this purpose, no doubt, 'to look carefully through' was enough, an avowal that gave great pleasure to his adversaries, who were just as sure of the purity of the orthodox faith, as Priestley was of its corruptions. For the greatest of all corruptions, according to Priestley, was the doctrine of the Trinity. He held that the doctrine of the divine unity was insisted upon by the whole system of revelation, but that gradually

> 'Christians have at length come to believe what they do not pretend to have any conception of, and than which it is not possible to frame a more express contradiction. For, while they consider Christ as the supreme, eternal God, the maker of heaven and earth, and of all things visible and invisible, they moreover acknowledge the Father and the Holy Spirit to be equally *God* in the same exalted sense, all three equal in power and glory, and yet all three constituting no more than one God.
>
> 'To a person the least interested in the inquiry, it must appear an object of curiosity to trace by what means, and by what steps, so great a change has taken place, and what circumstances in the history of other opinions, and of the world proved favourable to successive changes.' [1]

Priestley proceeded to trace the steps, and requested his readers to attend him with as much coolness and impartiality as he trusts he shall preserve through the whole inquiry.

It was not to be expected that such a bold attack on the doctrine of the Trinity should go unanswered. While at Dort, in Holland, the book was burnt, in this country the

[1] *Corruptions of Christianity*, Preface, p. 2.

challenge was taken up by Samuel Horsley, D.D., Archdeacon of St. Albans. In his charge to the clergy he warned them against Priestley's work. But the objects they aimed at were entirely different. Priestley wished to see the truth established, whatever it might be; Horsley merely tried to discredit his adversary. In the preface to the collected tracts, Horsley declared, 'it seems that the most effectual preservation against the intended mischief, would be to destroy the writer's credit and the authority of his name; which the fame of certain lucky discoveries in the prosecution of physical experiments had set high in popular esteem, by proof of his incompetency in every branch of literature connected with his present scheme; of which the work itself afforded evident specimens in great abundance'. And elsewhere Horsley wrote, 'Dr. Priestley forgets that the main argument with him and with me goes to different points. His point is the antiquity and the truth of the Unitarian doctrine. Mine is Dr. Priestley's incompetency in the subject.' [1] Thus the Archdeacon attacked inaccuracies of translations and his opponent's failure to understand Platonism, but he never defended the truth of the Trinity by rebutting Priestley's charges. Originally, Horsley declared, he believed that all the difficulties in the gospel were due to misinterpretation, but on reading Butler's *Analogy*, he concluded that mysteries were a necessity to religion. Thence he came to believe the pre-existence of Christ. 'Having once admitted his pre-existence in an exalted state, I saw the necessity of placing him at the head of the creation.' Though Horsley's method of obtaining faith might be gratifying to the orthodox, it is scarcely the historical method of arriving at true knowledge of the belief of the early Christians.

[1] Horsley, *Tracts in Controversy with Priestley*, p. 88.

Priestley enjoyed controversy, and believed that truth would appear the stronger from it. He attacked the Archdeacon with force, but not always with sweetness. Horsley was a clever opponent, keeping the argument as much as possible away from dangerous central truths, and attacking non-essentials. Like so many Church dignitaries, Horsley did not imitate the humility or the kindliness of the Galilean fishermen. To speak of the chapels where Priestley and Lindsey officiated as 'conventicles' was ill-mannered and not even legally correct. Priestley, on the other hand, would have done well to have paid no attention to such a childish insult.

At last, tired of the fray, considering himself victorious, Horsley retired with the reward of a bishopric, leaving others to dispute the field with his former antagonist. Horsley, wisely for the sake of his peace of mind, determined to read no more of Priestley, and the *History of the Early Opinions concerning Jesus Christ* was left untouched. Horsley rejoiced when bigotry and persecution drove Priestley to seek shelter beyond the Atlantic. But though the heretic might be fled, worse abounded in the form of atheism which Priestley had endeavoured to meet with a sane and rational faith. Samuel Rogers related that, 'Bishop Horsley one day met Monsey in the Park. "These are dreadful times!" said Horsley, 'not only do deists abound, but, would you think it, doctor?—some people deny that there is a God!"—"I can tell you," replied Monsey, "what is equally strange—some people believe that there are three".' [1]

Priestley was not silenced. If one history would not convert his opponents, he was prepared to publish another. So the *History of the Corruptions of Christianity* was followed by the *History of the Early Opinions*

[1] Rogers, *Table Talk*, p. 215.

concerning Jesus Christ. This, which has been considered
his best book, appeared in 1786.

In previous works Priestley had asserted that reason
was the only guide to the scriptures. In 1771, in his
pamphlet entitled, *An Appeal to the Candid and Earnest
Professors of Christianity*, he had said, 'Things *above* our
reason may, for anything that we know to the contrary,
be true, but things expressly *contrary* to our reason, as
that *three* should be *one*, or *one three*, can never appear to
be so'. In another place, Priestley tells a story of 'a good
old woman, who, on being asked whether she believed
the literal truth of *Jonah* being swallowed by the whale,
replied, yes, and added, that if the Scriptures had said
that *Jonah* swallowed the whale, she would have believed
it too'. Priestley's comment is, 'How a man can be said
to *believe* what is, in the nature of things, *impossible*, on
any authority, I cannot conceive'.[1] It was exactly the
same with the doctrine of the Trinity, which the *History
of the Early Opinions concerning Jesus Christ* aimed at
overthrowing. In the introduction, Priestley set out to
prove the doctrine of the Trinity unscriptural, but that
alone does not satisfy him. Even had it been found there,
he declared, 'it would have been impossible for a reasonable man to believe it, as it implies a contradiction, which
no miracles can prove.'[2] Further on he denies the obligation to believe any doctrine simply because an apostle held
it, unless miracles were performed which could prove its
truth.[3]

Like the *Corruptions of Christianity*, this history aimed
at tracing back the beliefs as far as they went. Priestley
held that the original opinions were those of the unlearned
classes, 'great bodies of men do not soon change their

---

[1] 'Letters to Candidates for Holy Orders'. *Works*, xviii., p. 507.
[2] Ibid. vi. 33, 34.   [3] Ibid. vi. 40.

opinions'.[1] The innovators were the learned, the philosophers well versed in Greek thought and Platonism.
Thus Priestley declared that the common people never
thought of Christ except as a man, and were Unitarians
until the time of Athanasius, or till after the Council of
Nice.[2] The innovation was the doctrine of the Trinity.

Almost twenty years earlier, Priestley had rejected the
doctrines of the Divinity and pre-existence of Christ; but
it is only now that he denied the doctrine of the miraculous
conception.[3] He takes great pleasure in showing all the
absurdities the early Fathers fell into, in explaining this
belief until they were content to allow that this profound
doctrine was hidden in mystery. Priestley must have read
extensively to make this work possible. His quotations
are copious and apposite, and he shows a certain sense of
the ridiculous in quoting from the Fathers far-fetched ex-
planations of theological absurdities. As in the *Corruptions of Christianity*, Priestley does not appear as an un-
biased judge, sifting the evidence, but as the zealous
advocate, making use of all the material he can lay hands
on to prove the point he is already convinced of.

Priestley's theological opinions show steady development; from Calvinism he passed to Arminianism, from
Arminianism to Arianism, and finally Socinianism. He
took up each new position because convinced of its truth.
Had the study of the early Fathers convinced him that his
opinions were wrong, he would have abandoned them. He
himself says that it was only in collecting material for the
Early Opinions that he came to disbelieve the doctrine of
the miraculous conception.[4] Had he found the evidence he
collected contrary to his belief in the humanity of Christ,
he would have rejected it as he had his faith in orthodoxy.

[1] *Works*, vi. 479.   [2] Ibid. vi. 490.   [3] Ibid. vi. 8.
[4] Ibid.

At the same time as Priestley was attacking the stronghold of orthodoxy, or so-called Christianity, he was also striking a blow for the simple faith of his Master against the forces of infidelity, championed as they were by David Hume and Edward Gibbon. Priestley saw that orthodoxy and infidelity were each other's best allies; the absurdities of the one driving men to the extremes of the other, and in turn its atheism drove the nervous to seek shelter within the sanctuary of mystery and authority. Against the two Priestley wished to set up Christianity in its original and purest form, which should be a way of life rather than a rule of observance and inflexible dogma.

The first part of the *Letters to a Philosophic Unbeliever* appeared in 1780, and was aimed in particular against the teaching of Hume. Priestley is less happy, and less successful in defending natural religion than in attacking orthodoxy. He repeats the usual arguments of design as evidence of an intelligent first cause.[1] He acknowledges the existence of an uncaused intelligent being to be difficult to conceive of, but not contrary to our experience.[2] Evil, again, is the stumbling-block in explaining a beneficent, almighty first cause. Priestley has already dealt with this subject in his *Disquisitions*, and here he treats it on similar lines. Pain and evil exist that greater good may arise from them; a state of discipline is necessary in this life to fit us for the next; improvement in this life is general, but the example Priestley chooses certainly seems unfortunate to a later generation. 'War is,' he declares, 'unspeakably less dreadful than formerly, though it is a great evil still.'[3] Further on Priestly notices the uses of evil. 'How could we be taught compassion for others,

---

[1] *Letters to a Philosophic Unbeliever*, p. 42.
[2] Ibid. 47.   [3] Ibid. 82.

without suffering ourselves, and where could the rudiments of the heroic virtues of fortitude, patience, clemency, &c., be acquired but in the school of adversity, in struggling with hardships and contending with oppression, ingratitude, and other vices; moral evils as well as natural ones?'[1] He compared Hume with Hartley, much to the former's loss. 'Compared with Dr. Hartley, I consider Mr. Hume as not even a child.'[2] Priestley was right in supposing that Hartley had a fuller idea of the Association of Ideas than had Hume. On the other hand, Priestley's criticism of Hume's theory of cause and effect is quite inadequate. To insert more links in the chain of cause and effect does not bring one nearer knowing why certain effects always follow certain causes.[3]

The second part of these Letters appeared in 1787 and was written in defence of revealed religion: at the same time Priestley wished to make it clear that it was only simple Christianity he was defending, for the corruptions were hindrances. The principal corruptions were 'a trinity of persons in the godhead, original sin, arbitrary predestination, atonement for the sins of men by the death of Christ, and (which has perhaps been as great a cause of infidelity as any other) the doctrine of the plenary inspiration of the scriptures'.[4] What therefore did Priestley suppose Christian faith to be? His answer is, 'a belief of all the great historical facts recorded in the Old and New Testament, in which we are informed of the creation and government of the world, the history of the discourses, miracles, death and resurrection of Christ, and his assurance of the resurrection of all the dead to a future life of retribution; and this is the doctrine that is of the most consequence, to enforce the good conduct of men'.[5]

[1] *Letters to a Philosophic Unbeliever*, pp. 97, 98.   [2] Ibid. 126.
[3] Ibid. i. 210.   [4] Ibid. ii. 33.   [5] Ibid. ii. 34.

But by denying plenary inspiration, and by scholarly criticism, Priestley was undermining those 'historical facts' relating to the creation and government of the world.

The last letter attacks Gibbon's chapters on the growth of Christianity. He considered Gibbon's explanation of the rise of Christianity quite inadequate, and that he dealt with secondary and not primary causes.

'For, without mentioning any more of his causes, to suppose that the inflexible or intolerant zeal of the primitive christians, and their firm belief in a future life, could have been produced without there being any truth in the history of the miracles, death, and resurrection of Christ, is to suppose that a pile of building must be supported by pillars, but that those pillars may stand in the air, without touching the ground; or with the Indians, that the world is supported by an elephant, and the elephant by a tortoise, but the tortoise by nothing.' [1]

Priestley accused Gibbons of misrepresenting the facts, and insinuating doubts as to the truths of those miracles which he so firmly believed.[2] At the time of the publication of the *History of the Corruptions of Christianity*, Priestley sent Gibbon a copy in the hope that he would enter into controversy with him, but Gibbon refused to be enticed, nor did he attempt to answer these Letters.

Priestley was not so absorbed in controversy that he could not take a part in public affairs. Naturally enough the slave trade received his attention, and he became a warm supporter of the abolitionist movement. Here for once he was working in harmony with his brethren of the Established Church. 'We are zealous and unanimous here',

1 Ibid. ii. 201.   2 Ibid. ii. 202.

he wrote in 1788, 'and next Sunday, previously to a town's meeting, we all preach on the subject (churches and meeting-houses alike), not to collect money, but to give information to such as may have been inattentive to the subject.'[1] Priestley thoroughly enjoyed being on the popular side. 'With the greatest satisfaction should I always *go with the multitude*, if a regard for the sacred rights of truth did not, on some occasions, forbid it.'[2]

But if, for once, Priestley had found himself on the popular side, he more often opposed it. In 1787 the Dissenters attempted to gain the repeal of the Test and Corporation Acts. Knowing his unpopularity, Priestley took no active part in the movement. Most unfortunately he had used metaphors of gunpowder and explosions to illustrate argument and the effect it would have on the Established Church. These remarks were now quoted in the House of Commons, with anything but a metaphorical sense. The petition for repeal was presented by Henry Beaufoy, member for Yarmouth, and, at one time, student at the Warrington Academy. Many of the members, no doubt, felt rather like Lord Chancellor Thurlow, when a deputation of Dissenting ministers waited upon him, in the hope of gaining his support. 'The Chancellor heard them very civilly, and then said, "Gentlemen, I'm against you, by G—— I am for the Established Church, d——mme! Not that I have any more regard for the Established Church than for any other church, but because *it is* established. And if you can get your d——d religion established, I'll be for that too.'[3] Pitt opposed the bill on grounds of expediency, and it consequently was rejected.

Having been quoted in the House of Commons,

---

[1] Rutt, ii. 7. [2] Preface to Sermon.
[3] Crabb Robinson, 378.

Priestley now thought he might reply. In his Letter to Pitt, he scolded the young prime minister, and pointed out his mistake in consulting the bishops, and remarked that, 'Bishops are recorded in all histories, as the most jealous, the most timorous, and of course the most vindictive of men.'

The Letters to Pitt were followed by *Familiar Letters to the Inhabitants of Birmingham.* Priestley thought he should reply to an attack made on him by the Rev. Martin Madan. He was now such a bugbear to the orthodox that they had almost persuaded themselves he was the devil. But if he really was as bad as Madan had made out, Priestley reminds him, 'he should not have trodden on my cloven hoof, or kicked me so near my tail, without remembering that I had horns and he had none'.

But Priestley was not on bad terms with all the clergymen of the Established Church. He had made friends with Doctor Samuel Parr, the great Whig, who needed a Boswell to have been as famous a conversationalist as Dr. Johnson. Parr remembered Priestley's friendship with all denominations. Years later, meeting a granddaughter of Priestley's, he said to her:

'Now remember this. I knew your grandfather, Dr. Priestley. He once invited me to dinner at Fairhill and I never was at a more agreeable party in my life. Your grandfather was at the head of the table, I sat at the bottom. At your grandfather's right was Mr. Berington, the Roman Catholic, and Mr. Galton, the Quaker, on his left. Next to me was Robert Robinson, the Baptist, and Mr. Proud, the minister of the New Jerusalem Church.' [1]

Priestley had thus managed to preserve his friendship

[1] *Royal Society MSS.*

with persons whose opinions he was attacking. Controversy and society were both dear to him. No doubt he hoped that this manner of life would last till the end. He had already noticed the storm which was gathering on the horizon of Europe, and which, in bursting, shattered his home along with mighty kingdoms.

CHAPTER X

THE FRENCH REVOLUTION AND THE BIRMINGHAM RIOTS

Bliss was it in that dawn to be alive,
But to be young was very Heaven!
Prelude, Book XI, lines 108, 109.

WHEN the French Revolution broke out, it was generally hailed as the dawning of a brighter day. Corruption, tyranny, and war were now about to disappear, and the reign of universal peace and brotherhood would begin. It was thought to be the advent of the millennium, when the lion should lie down with the lamb, and men would turn their swords into ploughshares. In England the Revolution was conceived as something similar to that experienced a hundred years earlier; the word 'revolution' had not yet come to summon up pictures of battle, murder, and sudden death. In the *Prelude* Wordsworth has depicted his own feelings, which were those of all ardent and generous youth.

Since the Revocation of the Edict of Nantes the life of the French Protestant had been precarious. Calas was broken on the wheel; the grandfather of Sir Samuel Romilly sought shelter in England; the Martineaus settled at Norwich. France was deprived of many of her sturdiest, bravest, most industrious and enterprising citizens. England was enriched by their settlement.

For a hundred years, the lot of the English Dissenter had been easy compared with that of the Huguenot. Now the positions were reversed. While in France there was religious equality, in England, under the Test and Corporation Acts, the Dissenter was deprived of full rights of citizenship, and, by law, the Unitarian was not even tolerated. No wonder then that the Revolution found some of its warmest supporters among the Dissenters.

Annually, on the fifth of November, the anniversary of the landing of William of Orange, the Revolution Society met to celebrate the glorious event of 1688. The Society consisted mostly of Dissenters, but a few Churchmen belonged. This year, 1789, it was decided that the celebrations should be more than usually impressive in honour of France. The old and venerable Dr. Price was chosen to preach the sermon. Its title was *The Love of our Country*, and the text 'Pray for the peace of Jerusalem. They shall prosper that love thee.' To promote their country's interest, he told his hearers, they should secure truth, virtue, and liberty. Liberty, as handed down to them from the Revolution, consisted in the right of conscience in religious matters; the right to resist power when abused; the right to choose their governors, to cashier them for misconduct, and to frame a government for themselves. English liberty was not complete so long as the Test Acts remained and parliamentary representation was a farce. Then Price thanked God that he had lived long enough to see thirty millions of people spurning slavery.[1] Happily for him, his 'Nunc dimittis' was heard and Price was rescued by death from the worst horrors of the English reign of terror.

Price had set rolling the ball of controversy. His sermon was the occasion of Burke's *Reflections on the French Revolution*. Burke, the friend of the American, now appeared as the enemy of the French Revolution. The *Reflections*, while containing much sound political philosophy, were built on a false assumption. Burke forgot that the elegance of the French court was bought at the expense of the peasants, sufferings too well authen-

[1] Cf. Brown, *Fr. Revolution.*

ticated in the travels of Arthur Young, by no means a
sympathizer with the Revolution. Tom Paine, the most
eloquent of his adversaries, summed up Burke's position
when he declared, 'He pities the plumage but forgets the
dying bird'.

Burke's *Reflections* appeared in 1790; and in the same
autumn, Priestley's reply which, in a year, went through
three editions. In it Priestley particularly attacked Burke's
remarks on the civil establishments of religion, 'a subject
not generally understood'.

'It is', Priestley wrote in the preface, 'with very
sensible regret that I find Mr. Burke and myself on
two opposite sides of any important question, and
especially that I must now no longer class him among
the friends of what I deem to be *the cause of liberty,
civil* or *religious*, after having, in a pleasing occasional
intercourse of many years, considered him in this
respectable light. In the course of his public life, he
has been greatly befriended by the Dissenters, many of
whom were enthusiastically attached to him; and we
always imagined that he was one on whom we could
depend, especially as he spoke in our favour in the
business of subscription, and he made a common cause
with us in zealously patronizing the liberty of America.

'That an avowed friend of the American revolution
should be an enemy to that of the French, which arose
from the same general principles, and in a great measure
sprung from it, is to me unaccountable. Nor is it much
less difficult to conceive how any person, who has had
America in his eye so long as Mr. Burke must necessarily
have contemplated it, could be so impressed, as he
appears to be, in favour of *ecclesiastical establishments*.
That country he sees to flourish as much as any other in
the annals of history, without any civil establishments

of religion at all. There he must see the civil government goes on very well without it. It neither stands in need of religion, nor does religion stand in need of it. For America is so far from being a country of atheists and unbelievers, that there is, I doubt not, a stronger general sense of religion there than in any other part of the world.

'In America also, and indeed in every other part of the known world, except the southern part of this island, Mr. Burke sees all civil offices open to persons of all religious persuasions without distinction, and without any inconvenience having been known to arise from it; and yet here he joins with a bigoted clergy, in rigorously confining them to the members of the established church. But even *this* is not so extraordinary as his not scrupling to class all the enemies of establishments with *cheats* and *hypocrites*, as if our opinions were so palpably absurd, that no honest man could possibly entertain them.

'Some are disposed to ascribe this change in Mr. Burke's views and politics, to his resentment of the treatment of the *coalition* by the Dissenters. And certainly so *sudden* an union of Mr. Burke and his friends with Lord North, with whom they had been in a state of violent opposition during the whole of the American war, did fill the Dissenters, but not the Dissenters only (for the shock affected the greater part of the nation) with horror. In this it is possible they might have judged wrong, listening to no *reason* against the effect of the first unfavourable *impression*; but they certainly acted from the best principles, an attachment to liberty, virtue, and consistency; and they lamented the fall of Mr. Burke, as that of a friend and a brother.

'However, the question before the reader, is not the

propriety or impropriety of any particular man's conduct, but the wisdom of great measures of government; as whether it be right and wise, to connect the business of *religion* with that of the *state,* in the manner in which it is done in this country, and whether the French nation is justifiable in their attempts to change their arbitrary form of government for another which they deem to be more favourable to their interests and natural rights.

'The question also with respect to *them,* is not whether they have taken the very best methods possible to gain their end, but whether the thing itself was worth their aiming at, and whether they have been those *very great fools* that Mr. Burke makes them to be. After all, mankind in general will judge by the event. If they succeed in establishing a free government, they will be applauded for their *judgement,* as well as for the *spirit* that they have shewn; and if they fail, they will be condemned for their precipitancy and folly. Thus every successful revolt is termed a revolution, and every unsuccessful one a rebellion.

'If the principles that Mr. Burke now advances (though it is by no means with perfect consistency) be admitted, mankind are always to be governed as they have been governed, without any inquiry into the *nature,* or *origin,* of their governments. The *choice of the people* is not to be considered, and though their happiness is aukwardly enough made by him the end of government; yet, having no choice, they are not to be judges of what is for their good. On these principles, the *church,* or the *state,* once established, must for ever remain the same. This is evidently the real scope of Mr. Burke's pamphlet, the principles of it being, in fact, no other than those of *passive obedience and non-resistance*, peculiar to the Tories and the friends of arbitrary power, such as were echoed from the pulpits of all the high church party, in the reigns of the Stuarts, and of Queen Anne. Let them, however, be produced again, and let us see in what manner they will be treated by the good sense and spirit of Englishmen at the present day.'

Priestley does not hesitate to lecture Burke, as he has Horsley and Pitt. 'You appear to me not to be sufficiently cool', he tells Burke rightly enough, 'to enter into this serious discussion. Your imagination is evidently heated, and your ideas confused. The objects before you do not appear in their proper shapes and colours.'[1] Burke 'should not blame the framers of the new government, but the wretched state of the old one, and those who brought it into that state'.[2] As Sully and Burke himself[3] had said before, Priestley declared 'A whole people is not apt to revolt, till oppression has become extreme, and been long continued, so that they despair of any other remedy than that desperate one'.[4] Burke, he says, is unjust in holding the National Assembly guilty of all the murders that have occurred, and more unjust in describing 'Dr. Price as exulting in the above-mentioned horrid outrages, which, I dare say, give him much more serious concern than they do you, and for a very obvious reason. He wishes to recommend the revolution, and therefore is sorry for every thing that disgraces it; whereas you wish to discredit it'.[5]

Burke's defence of the power of the Crown, Priestley thought, might be construed as high treason under two Acts of Parliament of the 4th and 6th of Queen Anne,

---

[1] *Letters to Burke,* 3rd edition, p. 2.   [2] Ibid. 4.
[3] *Thoughts on the Cause of Our Present Discontents.*
[4] *Letters to Burke,* p. 7.   [5] Ibid. 21.

whereby it was enacted that it was high treason to maintain by writing or printing, 'that the kings and queens of this realm, with and by the authority of Parliament, are not able to make laws and statutes of sufficient validity, to limit the crown, and the descent, inheritance, and government thereof'.[1] Apparently the idea was not peculiar to Priestley, though he realized it was absurd, for he wrote to Lindsey: 'Lord Stanhope can hardly be serious in his design to impeach Mr. Burke of high treason'.[2]

Burke had compared Price with the regicide, Hugh Peters. Though not defending Peters' conduct, Priestley declared that the execution of Charles the First was a good thing. 'The *thirtieth of January* was (to use a phrase of Admiral Keppel's) a *proud day* for England, as well as the *fourteenth of July* for France; and it will be remembered as such by the latest posterity of *freemen*. Let all tyrants read the history of both, and tremble. Good princes will read it without any unpleasant emotion.'[3]

Burke was guilty of confounding 'the idea of religion itself, with that of the civil establishment of it;[4] Priestley maintained that religion required no such support, and 'that its beneficial operation is injured by such establishment, and the more in proportion to its riches'. And since 'the state has a right to dispose of *all* property within itself' it may quite well utilize the wealth of the church.[5] Burke's love of the established order would lead him to worship in St. Peter's at Rome, in Sancta Sophia at Constantinople, but he could never have entered into a place where Peter or Paul would have been allowed to preach.[6]

Priestley realized that Burke did not always see below the surface. 'But amusing yourself with the *shadow*, you

[1] Quoted ibid. 36. [2] Rutt, ii. 97. [3] *Letters to Burke*, p. 48.
[4] Ibid. 52. [5] Ibid. 53. [6] Ibid. 61.

wholly neglect the *substance*.'¹ The Established Church was a hindrance to religion and as such should be got rid of.

'Now, when I see this *fungus* of an *establishment* upon the noble plant of *christianity*, draining its best juices; when I see this *Sloth* upon its stately branches, gnawing it, and stripping it bare; or, to change my comparison, when I see the *Glutton* upon the shoulders of this noble animal, the blood flowing down, its very vitals in danger; if I wish to preserve the tree, or the animal, must I not, without delay, extirpate the fungus, destroy the Sloth, and kill the Glutton. Indeed, Sir, say, or write, what you please, such vermin deserve no mercy. You may stand by, and weep for the fate of your favourite fungus, your Sloth, or your Glutton, but I shall not spare them.'²

Priestley again foretells the near end of the church.

'The spirit of free and rational inquiry is now abroad, and without any aid from the powers of this world, will not fail to overturn all error and false religion, wherever it is found, and neither the church of Rome, nor the church of England, will be able to stand before it.'³

The Church in danger, Priestley declared, was a cry as old as the Church itself, and was but an excuse for the spoliation of others; a statement that the next year proved only too true. But:

'the *church of Christ* is built upon a rock, and we are assured that *the gates of hell shall not prevail against it*. Now, had this church of yours, whose fears and cries have always been the signal of alarm to all its neigh-

---

¹ *Letters to Burke*, p. 68.   ² Ibid. 84.   ³ Ibid. 113, 114.

bours, been made of proper materials, and constructed in a proper manner, had it been built upon this rock of *truth*, it would never have had anything to fear. Its own evidence and excellence would have supported it. Should the *state* itself be overturned, the people would, of themselves, and from predilection, reinstate their favourite *church* in all its former rights and privileges. But you are sensible it has not this hold on the minds of the people, and you justly suspect that, if any misfortune should happen to it, they would never rebuild it, but, if left to their own free choice, would adopt some other plan, more useful and commodious.' [1]

A better and happier period in the world's history is at hand.

'Together with the general prevalence of true principles of civil government, we may expect to see the extinction of all *national prejudice* and enmity, and the establishment of *universal peace* and goodwill among all nations.' [2]

Discussion of differences will lead the minority to give way.

'The empire of reason will ever be the reign of peace. This, Sir, will be the happy state of things distinctly and repeatedly foretold in many prophecies, delivered more than two thousand years ago; when the common parent of mankind will *cause wars to cease to the ends of the earth*, when *men shall beat their swords into ploughshares, and their spears into pruning hooks; when nation shall no more rise up against nation, and when they shall learn war no more.* Is. ii. 4, Micah iv. 3. This is a state of things which good sense, and the prevailing spirit of commerce, aided by christianity, and true philosophy,

---

[1] Ibid. 123–4.   [2] Ibid. 146.

cannot fail to effect in time. But it can never take place
while mankind are governed in the wretched manner
in which they now are. For peace can never be established, but upon the extinction of the causes of war.' [1]

By 1791 party feeling ran high. Burke and Fox had
severed their friendship in a famous scene in the House of
Commons. The Revolution had already begun to disgrace itself. Thus, perhaps, it was unwise to choose to
celebrate the 14th of July. As yet there existed no properly
organized police force capable of protecting an unpopular
minority. London had, in 1780, experienced the horror of
a mob at large when the Gordon Riots had only been
suppressed by the use of the military at the King's especial
command. In Birmingham feeling ran particularly high
between Churchman and Dissenter, Tory and Whig.
But the friends of the Revolution were not to be deterred
and they decided to celebrate July 14th with a dinner.
On the 11th the following advertisement appeared in the
Birmingham Gazette.

Hotel. Birmingham, July 7, 1791.

Commemoration of the French Revolution.

'A number of Gentlemen intend DINING together on
the 14th instant, to commemorate the auspicious day
which witnessed the Emancipation of Twenty-six
Millions of People from the yoke of Despotism, and
restored the blessings of equal Government to a truly
great and enlightened Nation, with whom it is our
interest as a commercial People, and our Duty, as
Friends to the General Rights of Mankind, to promote
a free intercourse, as subservient to a permanent
Friendship.

'Any Friend to Freedom, disposed to join this

[1] *Letters to Burke,* p. 150.

intended temperate Festivity, is desired to leave his Name at the Bar of the Hotel, where Tickets may be had at 5s. each, including a Bottle of Wine, but no person will be admitted without one.

∴ Dinner will be on the Table at Three o'clock precisely.' [1]

Immediately beneath this advertisement was placed another.

'*On Friday next will be published,*

Price ONE HALFPENNY,

AN AUTHENTIC List of all those who Dine at the Hotel, in Temple-Row, Birmingham on Thursday, the 14th instant, in Commemoration of the French Revolution.

Vivant Rex et Regina.' [2]

This should have been sufficient warning that mischief was afoot. Then to add to the excitement the following handbill was secretly printed and circulated.

'*My Countrymen,*

The second year of Gallic Liberty is nearly expired. At the commencement of the third, on the 14th of this month, it is devoutly to be wished, that every enemy to civil and religious despotism would give sanction to the *majestic common cause* by a public celebration of the anniversary. Remember that on the 14th of July the Bastille, that "High Altar and Castle of Despotism" fell. Remember the enthusiasm *peculiar* to the cause of Liberty, with which it was attacked. Remember that generous humanity that taught the oppressed, groaning under the weight of insulted rights, to save the lives of the oppressors! Extinguish the mean prejudices of

---

[1] Langford, i. 477-8.   [2] Ibid. 478.

nations; and let your numbers be collected, and sent as a free-will offering to the National Assembly.

'But is it possible to forget that your own Parliament is venal? Your Minister hypocritical? Your Clergy legal oppressors? The reigning Family extravagant? The Crown of a certain great Personage becoming every day too weighty for the head that wears it? Too weighty for the people who *gave* it? Your taxes partial and excessive? Your representation a cruel *insult* upon the sacred rights of property, religion, and freedom?

'But on the 14th of this month, prove to the political sycophants of the day, that You reverence the Olive Branch; that You *will* sacrifice to public tranquillity, till the majority *shall* exclaim, *The Peace of Slavery is worse than the War of Freedom.* Of that moment let Tyrants beware.' [1]

In spite of proffered rewards the writer was never apprehended, and whether he was an over ardent friend of liberty or a designing Tory, writing to incite the mob, has never been decided. If a Tory, he was very clever as well as wicked. Yet the advice to remain tranquil for the present is scarcely likely to have occurred to a man whose one object was to raise, as quickly as possible, a bloody riot. On the other hand, it should be remembered that forged letters of a treasonous nature were found in Priestley's house, having been put there particularly to anger the mob.

But when they who intended to dine on the 14th wished to deny the authorship of the handbill, they declared once more their support of the Revolution.

'*Birmingham Commemoration of the French Revolution.*

'Several handbills having been circulated in the town, which can only be intended to create distrust concern-

[1] *Appeal to the Public,* i, Appendix I.

ing the intention of the meeting, to disturb its harmony, and influence the minds of the people, the gentlemen who proposed it think it necessary to declare their entire disapprobation of all such handbills, and their ignorance of the authors.

'Sensible themselves of a free government, they rejoice in the extension of Liberty to their Neighbours; and at the same time avowing, in the most explicit manner, their *firm attachment* to the *Constitution of their own Country*, as vested in the Three Estates of *King*, *Lords* and *Commons*. Surely no Free-born Englishman can refrain from exulting in this addition to the general mass of happiness! It is the Cause of Humanity! It is the Cause of the People!' [1]

It seems certain that their enemies premeditated some mischief against the friends of the Revolution, or at least that the High Church party meant to injure the Dissenters, and more particularly the Presbyterian or Unitarian Dissenters. At one moment it seemed wise to the supporters of the dinner that they should abandon it, but on the assertion of the hotel proprietor that the excitement was overrated, they decided to hold it.

On July 13th William Russell, a principal citizen of Birmingham and the right hand man of the New Meeting, met Carles, one of the magistrates, slightly drunk, who assured his Presbyterian friend that he would not have a hair of his head injured. Later having learnt that a meeting had been held at the house of a church-and-king partisan 'for the purpose of considering how to punish those damn'd presbyterians',[2] Russell concluded that Carles and the other magistrates knew mischief was brewing, and were ready to save the lives, but not the property, of the Dissenters.

[1] Langford, i. 479.   [2] *Appeal to the Public*, ii. 121.

On the night of the dinner the magistrates dined in town to watch events and be there if needed, so they said. But if circumstances needed their presence on the spot, they also required the swearing in of additional constables. The dinner was attended by about eighty persons. The chair was taken by Captain Keir, a Churchman whose house was not sought out for spoliation. Toasts were drunk, the first being 'The King and Constitution', and all the toasts were harmless enough. It was not the kind of meeting, composed as it was, of middle class, middle-aged Dissenters and Churchmen, where the toast mentioned in *The Times*[1] could have been drunk: 'Destruction to the present government—and the king's head upon a charger', a toast which later was attributed to Priestley's proposal, though he did not attend the dinner. The dinner broke up early, and with the exception of some booing on arrival and departure, the diners dispersed quietly to their homes.

About eight o'clock the crowd again gathered round the hotel and smashed its windows. Then some one started the cry of 'To the New Meeting', and the crowd immediately took itself there, where it began the work of destruction; fire was set to the building and it was very soon reduced to a shell. Mr. Curtis, one of the clergymen of the Established Church in Birmingham, was accused of having taken the key of the fire engine from its usual place and left it in the hands of his clerk with the strict injunction not to give it up. When applied to for the key his clerk repeated his orders, and when forced to part with the key wrote a letter to Curtis explaining his necessity.[2] From the New Meeting the crowd went to the Old, where they continued their work of destruction. In each case the leaders of the mob, for it was never denied that

[1] July 19th, 1791, quoted in *Appeal to the Public*, i, App. III.   [2] Ibid. ii. 51.

there were leaders, though their identity remained un-known, were careful to make sure that no general con-flagration was begun.

Meantime what were the magistrates doing? On the most favourable authority, nothing; on less favourable, they were encouraging the rioters, who believed that their conduct was pleasing to those in authority.

When the two Meetings were destroyed, the cry went up 'To Dr. Priestley's', and thither the mob set off. Priestley had spent the day quietly at home. After dinner the Russells had called and told him how satisfactory the dinner had been; after supper he was preparing to amuse himself with a game of backgammon when some young men arrived with the news that the mob was at the work of destruction, and that it intended to attack the Doctor's house. Priestley scarcely believed this, but was persuaded to go to a neighbour's house a little farther out of town.

'At this moment', he wrote, 'which was about half past nine o'clock, Mr. S. Ryland, a friend of mine, came with a chaise, telling us there was no time to lose, but that we must immediately get into it, and drive off. Ac-cordingly, we got in with nothing more than the clothes we happened to have on, and drove from the house. But hearing that the mob consisted only of people on foot, and concluding that when they found I was gone off in a chaise, they could not tell whither, they would never think of pursuing me, we went no farther than Mr. Russell's, a mile on the same road, and there we continued several hours, Mr. Russell himself, and other persons, being upon the road, on horseback to get intelligence of what was passing. I also more than once walked about half way back to my own house for the same purpose; and then I saw the fires from the two meeting-houses, which were burning down.

'About twelve, we were told that some hundreds of the mob were breaking into my house, and that when they had demolished *it*, they would certainly proceed to Mr. Russell's. We were persuaded, therefore, to get into the chaise again, and drive off; but we went no farther than Mr. Thomas Hawkes' on Moseley-Green, which is not more than half-a-mile farther from the town, and there we waited all the night.

'It being remarkably calm, and clear moon-light, we could see to a considerable distance, and being upon a rising ground, we distinctly heard all that passed at the house, every shout of the mob, and almost every stroke of the instruments they had provided for breaking the doors and furniture. For they could not get any fire, though one of them was heard to offer two guineas for a lighted candle; my son, whom we left behind us, having taken the precaution to put out all the fires in the house, and others of my friends, got all the neighbours to do the same. I afterwards heard that much pains was taken, but without effect, to get fire from my large electrical machine, which stood in the library.

'About three o'clock in the morning the noises ceased, and Mr. Russell and my son coming to us, said that the mob was almost dispersed, that not more than twenty of them remained, and those so much intoxicated, that they might easily be taken. We therefore returned with him, and about four o'clock were going to bed at his house. But when I was undressing myself for that purpose, news came that there was a fresh accession of some hundreds more to the mob, and that they were advancing towards Mr. Russell's. On this we got into the chaise once more, and driving through a part of the town distant from the mob, we went to Dudley, and then to my son-in-law's, Mr.

Finch, at Heath-Forge, five miles farther, where we arrived before breakfast, and brought the first news of our disaster.

'Here I thought myself perfectly safe, and imagining that when the mischief was over (and I had no idea of its going beyond my own house) and supposing that as the people in general would be ashamed, and concerned, at what had happened, I might return; thinking also that the area within the walls of the meeting-house might soon be cleared, I intended, if the weather would permit, to preach there the Sunday following, and from this text, *Father forgive them, for they know not what they do.*

'At noon, however, we had an express from Stourbridge, to acquaint us that the mob had traced me to Dudley, and would pursue me to Heath. To this I paid no attention, nor to another from Dudley in the evening to inform us of the same thing; and being in want of sleep, I went to bed soon after ten. But at eleven I was awaked, and told that a third express was just arrived from Dudley, to assure us that some persons were certainly in pursuit of me, and would be there that night. All the family believing this, and urging me to make my escape, I dressed myself, got on horseback, and with a servant rode to Bridgnorth, where I arrived about two in the morning.

'After about two hours' sleep in this place, I got into a chaise, and went to Kidderminster, on my way to London. Here I found myself among friends, and, as I thought, far enough from the scene of danger, especially as we continually heard news from Birmingham, and that the mischief did not extend beyond the town. Hearing, particularly, that all was quiet at Dudley, I concluded that there could be no real cause

M

of apprehension at Heath; and being unwilling to go farther than was necessary, I took a horse, and arrived there in the evening.

'There, however, I found the family in great consternation at the sight of me; and Mr. Finch just arriving from Dudley, and saying that they were in momentary expectation of a riot there, that the populace were even assembled in the street, and were heard to threaten the meeting-house, the house of the minister, and those of other principal Dissenters, and that all attempts to make them disperse had been in vain, I mounted my horse again, though much fatigued, and greatly wanting sleep.

'My intention was to get to an inn about six miles on the road to Kidderminster, where I might get a chaise, and in it proceed to that town. No chaise, however, was to be had; so that I was under the necessity of proceeding on horseback, and neither the servant nor myself distinguishing the road in the night, we lost our way, and at break of day found ourselves on Bridgnorth race ground, having ridden nineteen miles, till we could hardly sit our horses.

'Arriving at this place a second time, about three o'clock in the morning, we with some difficulty roused the people at an indifferent inn, and I immediately got into bed, and slept a few hours. After breakfast we mounted our horses, and I got a second time to Kidderminster. There, finding that if I immediately took a chaise, and drove fast, I might get to Worcester time enough for the mail-coach, I did so; and meeting with a young man of my own congregation, he accompanied me thither, which was a great satisfaction to me, as he acquainted me with many particulars of the riot, of which I was before ignorant. At Worcester I was just time enough for the coach, and fortunately there was one place vacant. I took it, and travelling all night, I got to London on Monday morning, July 18th.' [1]

Priestley was by no means the only victim of this reign of terror. The Russells were fellow sufferers, and one of them, Martha, later in life, wrote down her recollections of these days. She was much impressed by Priestley's behaviour.

'No human being', she wrote, 'could, in my opinion, appear in any trial more like divine, or show a nearer resemblance to our Saviour, than he did then. Undaunted he heard the blows which were destroying the house and laboratory that contained all his valuable and rare apparatus and their effects, which it had been the business of his life to collect and use. . . . Not one hasty or impatient expression, not one look expressive of murmur or complaint, not one tear or sigh escaped him; resignation and a conscious innocence and virtue seemed to subdue all these feelings of humanity.' [2]

The Russells' own experiences were scarcely preferable to Doctor Priestley's. When the Priestleys left them hurriedly at 4 o'clock on the Friday morning, the Russells set about packing up.

'The neighbourhood had by this time become all alarmed for us, and our poor neighbours for miles round were coming all through the day, requesting to assist us in packing and to carry some of our things to their cottages, in order to secure them for us. Our house was filled with people from top to bottom, some packing one thing, some another, some hiding things about our own premises, others taking them to a barn fixed upon as a place of safety and secrecy, and others

[1] *Appeal to the Public*, i. 29–33. [2] *Christian Reformer*, May, 1835.

again to their own homes, and thus endangering themselves by a risk of their being discovered, and suffering, in consequence, from the blind fury of the mob.'

The young Russells took refuge with a neighbour.

'Accordingly, we loaded ourselves with cold meat pies &c., and set off, intending to take up our quarters there till all was over, thinking we should be near to hear how things went and could profit by circumstances as they arose. As we passed across the fields, we were alarmed by parties of men in their shirt sleeves, without hats, all half-drunk; they were breaking the boughs from the trees and hedges, shouting, laughing, swearing and singing in a manner that seemed hideous beyond expression. After much alarm and frequently hiding ourselves behind the hedges and trees, we at length arrived at our place of destination.'

Meanwhile Mr. Russell was trying to make the magistrates act, but could get no reply to his letters. The Russells were now sent five miles farther on where they stayed till Saturday evening at 10, when

'all of a sudden the dreadful shouts of the mob assailed our ears, and almost at the same instant two women came running as if for their lives and quite out of breath; they begged us for God's sake to get away, for that the mob were coming, they would be there immediately, and their fury was ungovernable. Such a scene of confusion now followed as cannot be told; all ran about as if not knowing what to do or where to go; there were seven or eight young children in the house, some were wrapped up in blankets, others taken from their beds as they were, all ran out of the house, but knew not whither to turn their steps.'

The Russells now set off to walk to Alcester as fast as they could, with the noise of the mob in their ears. On the public road they heard horsemen behind them, and hid. As the riders passed them the Russells heard one of them say, 'I know there 's a d——d Presbyterian somewhere hereabouts, we'll have him before morning', and knew this was meant to apply to their father. But walking on they did not see that the horsemen had stopped until it was too late to hide, and there was nothing to do but to go on and look as unconcerned as possible,

'accordingly, we passed them, they looked hard at us but said nothing, and presently galloped up and re-passed us, then stopped their horses till we again passed them, and this they continued to do in such a manner, that each of us was alive to secret apprehensions. . . . We continued thus for about three miles, marching with firm pace, but with almost a deadly silence: the moon shone uncommonly bright, the shadows it cast were therefore unusually strong, and almost every shade from a tree or bush that fell across our path startled us. The men on horseback were sometimes by our side, sometimes out of sight, behind us, sometimes before; their intentions we feared, and our situation powerfully aided our apprehensions. After a little time we now heard a horse coming after us and were at first alarmed, but afterwards relieved by finding it was our own servant, who had gone to C.'s, and not finding us there, had rode after us. He informed us of the truth of our conjectures, for that our house was burnt, and all the gardens and premises most dreadfully laid waste. Though he brought us this sad intelligence, we were all truly relieved to see him and keep him with us as a guard from these men. Shortly after we met my father in the greatest distress; his fears for us had almost distracted him; he had set out to meet us, and by some unlucky chance his horse had got away from him, and to get him again had taken him a long time, and almost exhausted his remaining strength; he had just caught him as we came up, and our meeting was joyful and happy, though under such sad circumstances. My father now sent the servant back, with orders to have our chaise sent to meet us at Stratford, as he had resolved to go straight up to London and remonstrate with Mr. Pitt on these outrageous proceedings. My father now accompanying us, we now continued our route comparatively speaking with pleasure, for the men had gone on before us since William joined us, and we saw nothing more of them. We now passed several houses, at the door of each the family was collected in a solemn sort of silence; they all gazed at us as we passed; not a word was spoken, except sometimes by some of them in a whisper. We held our peace, not knowing whether any we might address or put any questions to, were friends or enemies. In about half-an-hour, we met an honest and respectable farmer, a brother to one of my father's tenants, who had heard of our being in the neighbourhood, and had set out to see for, and assist us; he accompanied us the remainder of our walk, and when we arrived at the end of the seven miles, which in the afternoon we had imagined it quite impossible for us to accomplish, we found ourselves sufficiently strong to walk another seven. On entering our inn, we were much disturbed to find it filled with riotous people, and to observe, just before we came up, the very same men who had tormented us, go in before us. We found here my father's tenant, the brother of the man who met us, and, on relating to him the circumstances of the men who had followed us, we requested him to go into the kitchen and see if he knew them, or could gather any thing from their conversation: this he did, and in a short time returned, informing us he knew them, and that one of them was the most violent man in all the county and a most profligate creature. This being the case, we could not think of remaining here, lest they should discern my father, and begged he would permit us to walk to Alcester, eight miles farther, where we could get a hired chaise and proceed to Stratford. At first, he would not hear of it, but insisted upon our staying there and taking some rest and refreshment, as a good supper and beds were provided: though so much exhausted, yet in our state of mind these were no temptations to us; I felt able to walk twenty miles farther, and would infinitely rather have done it than have remained in that house. The Mr. G—— we had first met requested we would go on to his house, about two miles farther off, and wait there whilst he went to Alcester and brought a chaise to us. This was determined upon, when, just as we were setting off, up came our coach, which had been left at B. C.'s with Mr. L—'s family in: this was very fortunate; they took possession of the rooms and supper that had been prepared for us, and we got into our coach, drawn by a pair of horses neither of which had ever been in a carriage before, and the tenant we had met at this house for a coachman, who had never drove a carriage before. Our faithful little dog, as if fearful of being left behind, jumped into the carriage before us, and we all stepped in, thinking it the greatest luxury we had ever enjoyed. We arrived safe at Mr. G—'s, and he not being arrived with the chaise, we took some refreshment offered us by the good lady, and at her earnest request went upstairs to get a little repose. Here, a curious scene presented itself; we three ladies were shown into a room with four beds in all, and all but one, whether occupied by men or women we did not know; but the loud nasal concert, and the different notes of which it was composed, seemed to indicate both: we were amused at our situation, and felt sufficiently at ease to laugh at it. We lay down upon the bed, and our faithful little dog by our side; but the room was suffocatingly hot and the number of persons in it made the air very oppressive: this, together with the music that assailed our ears and a most numerous swarm of fleas, which attacked us all, kept rest and even quiet at a distance.' [1]

At length a carriage arrived from Alcester and the Russell family got into it. At four in the morning they arrived at Stratford, where they got into their own chaise and with hired horses started for London. At one time the post boy was so drunk that Mr. Russell had to drive. At last, on Monday morning, July 18th, about seven o'clock they arrived at Bates's Hotel in the Adelphi. 'On sitting down here for the first time since Thursday had we thought ourselves safe or at rest. Now we found both, and the greatest refreshment from washing off the dust and filth from our skins and in changing our clothes.' That night, tired out, they went to bed early, but were awakened by hearing a great noise which they supposed to be the mob, which they imagined had followed them to London. But they were assured the noise was caused only by the Covent Garden porters, so, 'smiling at our own fears, we returned to comfortable rest'.

Meanwhile, at Birmingham, the mob continued its work of destruction. Priestley's house, which he re-

[1] *Christian Reformer*, May, 1835.

fused to have defended, had been destroyed with its library, laboratory, its valuable apparatus. His letters were scattered about and read by all and every one who chose.

'On Friday morning, as they recovered from the fatigue and intoxication of the preceding night, different parties of the rioters entered the town to the great consternation of all the inhabitants. The doors of every place of confinement were thrown open, and they paraded through the streets, armed with bludgeons, loudly vociferating "Church and King!", words which all the inhabitants now chalked upon their window shutters and doors for the security of their dwellings.'[1]

Apparently the magistrates now tried, 'by the most conciliating language, to induce them to separate, and desist from further violence', but they had lost control and the mob was mad with its orgy. So in the afternoon 'the elegant mansion of Mr. John Riland', once the home of Baskerville, was attacked by the rioters and set on fire.

'Here many of them were so insensible of their danger that the flames caught them in the upper chambers, and others were in such a state of intoxication that they could not be drawn from, but perished in the cellar. Three, most terribly scorched and bruised, were conveyed to the Hospital; seven ladies, so much disfigured that they could hardly be recognized, have been dug out of the ruins; and a man, on Monday (who had been immuned in one of the vaults), worked his way out. He lived only to say, he knew by the groans that he heard that several had expired in a worse situation than——and he expired as they laid him upon the grass.'[2]

---

[1] *Birmingham Gazette*, as quoted in Langford, i. 482.   [2] Ibid. i. 483.

Now at last the magistrates swore in additional constables, but the time had gone by when a few could have dispelled the excited mob. Throughout Saturday and Sunday the burning of the homes of the Dissenters went on.

'The terror and distress which pervaded the whole town on Saturday, while these dreadful scenes were acting, will be better conceived than described. The Magistrates had tried every means of persuasion to no effect; large bills were stuck up requesting all persons to retire to their respective homes, to no purpose; and numbers of the rioters, now joined by thieves and drunken prostitutes from every quarter, were, with blue cockades in their hats, in all parts of the Town, and in small bodies levying contributions on the inhabitants. There was scarcely a house-keeper that dared refuse them meat, drink, money, or whatever they demanded.' [1]

The handbills circulated by the magistrates were so conciliatory that it was easy enough for the victims to believe that the magisterial authority had been wielded in a half-hearted fashion. These were the notices they posted.

Birmingham, July 16th, 1791.

'Friends and Fellow Countrymen,

'It is earnestly requested that every *true friend* to the *Church of England*, and to the laws of his country, will reflect how much a *continuance* of the present proceedings must injure *that Church* and *that King they are intended to support*; and how highly unlawful it is to destroy the rights and property of *any* of our neighbours. And all *true friends* to the town and trade of Birmingham, *in particular*, are entreated to forbear *immediately* from all

[1] *Birmingham Gazette*, as quoted in Langford, i. 484.

riotous and violent proceedings; dispersing and returning peaceably to their trades and callings, as the
only way to do *credit to themselves* and *their cause*, and
to promote the peace, happiness, and prosperity of this
great and flourishing town.' [1]

And:

Birmingham, Sunday July 17th, 1791.

'*Important Information to the Friends of Church and
King.*

'Friends and Fellow Churchmen,

'Being convinced you are unacquainted, that the
great losses which are sustained by *your burning* and
destroying of the houses of so many individuals, will
eventually fall upon the *county at large*, and not upon
the persons to whom they belonged, we feel it our duty
to inform you that the damages already done, upon the
best computation that can be made, will amount to
One Hundred Thousand Pounds; the whole of which
enormous sum will be charged upon the respective
parishes and paid out of the rates. We, therefore, as
your *friends*, conjure you immediately to desist from
the destruction of *any more houses*; otherwise the very
proceedings of your zeal for showing your attachment
to the CHURCH and KING, will inevitably be the means
of most seriously injuring innumerable families who
are hearty supporters of Government, and bring on an
addition of taxes, which *yourselves, and the rest of the
Friends of the Church*, will for years feel a very grievous
burden.

'This we assure you was the case in London, when
there were so many houses, and public buildings burnt
and destroyed in the year 1780, and you may rely upon

[1] *Appeal to the Public*, i. 148.

it, will be the case on the present occasion. And we must observe to you, that *any further* violent proceedings will more offend your King and Country than serve the cause of Him and the Church.

'*Fellow Churchmen*, as you love your King, regard his laws, and restore peace.

GOD SAVE THE KING.

Aylesford	*J. Carless*
E. Finch	*B. Spencer*
Robert Lawley	*H. Gres. Lewis*
Robert Lawley, Jun.	*Charles Curtis*
R. Moland	*Spencer Madan*
W. Digby	*Edward Palmer*
Edward Carver	*W. Villers*
John Brooke	*W. W. Mason.*' [1]

On Sunday evening the first detachment of troops arrived to the great relief of all law-abiding citizens. Order was at once established. The next task for those in authority was to bring the participants to justice.

It has never yet been decided how far the magistrates were responsible for the riots. The Dissenters swore affidavits accusing the justices of not merely making no attempts to subdue the rioters, but actually by their presence, encouraging them. It was said that Dr. Spencer, one of the magistrates, and a clergyman of the Established Church, was present at the destruction by the rioters of Priestley's house, 'and instead of reading the riot act, or taking any steps to disperse them, he called several of them to him, and made them huzza, and join with him in the shout of 'Church and King'; he then said, 'you have done very well what you have done; don't hurt the house; it does not belong to Dr. Priestley; it belongs to Mr.

---

[1] *Appeal to the Public*, i. 148, 149.

Lloyd, a Quaker, a gentleman respected by all that know him.' One of the mob said it belonged to Squire Taylor; another said it belonged to somebody else; but several cried out that 'it belonged to the Presbyterians, and it shall come down!' Dr. Spencer then retired, and when he was departing, said, 'Take care and do not hurt one another.' At the burning of the meeting-houses rioters were heard declaring 'To the New Meeting, Justice Carles will protect us'—'Justice Carles sent us down here'—'Damn me! the justices say we may pull down the meetings, but not hurt any body's property'—'the justices will protect us'. [1]

The following year Whitbread proposed that an inquiry should be held into the conduct of the magistrates, but was opposed by the Government. The Government's attitude no doubt was similar to that of George III who had written to Dundas: 'Though I cannot but feel better pleased that Priestley is the sufferer for the doctrines he and his party have instilled, and that the people see them in their true light, yet I cannot approve of their having employed such atrocious means of showing their discontent.' [2]

Attempts were made to bring the rioters to justice. Out of 2,000 twenty were apprehended. Of these, thirteen alone were tried, of whom five were found guilty; three of them were executed and two pardoned.

The trials were a travesty of justice, the slightest excuse being enough to gain an acquittal. Thus one of the accused had been seen driving off some pigs, but was exculpated when his sister assured the jury that his object had been to save them. A Birmingham jury became a byword for leniency. 'A gentleman', Hutton related,

[1] *Parliamentary History.* Debate on Mr. Whitbread's Motion respecting the Riots at Birmingham, May 21st, 1792.   [2] Langford, i. 477.

'soon after this, hunting with Mr. Corbett's fox hounds, was so sure of killing the fox, that he cried, "Nothing but a Birmingham jury can save him!".' [1]

The compensation claimed by the sufferers in the riots amounted to £35,095 13*s*. 6*d*. £26, 961 2*s*. 3*d*. was recovered at the expense of £13,000.[2] No wonder Priestley and others despaired of British justice.

Not all members of the Established Church approved of the outrages of the mob. At a public dinner

'Dr. Parr was called on to drink "Church and King". At first, he resolutely declined. But the obligation of compliance being urgently pressed upon him—rising at length, with firmness and dignity—with a manner of impressive solemnity, and with a voice of powerful energy, he spoke thus—"I am compelled to drink the toast given from the chair; but I shall do so with my own comment. Well, then, gentlemen—Church and King.—Once it was the toast of Jacobites; now it is the toast of incendiaries. It means a church without the gospel— and a king above the laws!" ' [3]

Most men were not so brave as Parr. Till he went to America, Priestley found, outside of his own circle, unkindness and hostility. The only non-political, non-religious society which sent him condolences was the Philosophical Society of Derby! Even some of the Fellows of the Royal Society turned their backs on him.[4]

Priestley intended to return to Birmingham, and was prepared to preach his sermon on forgiveness. But feeling ran high and his friends believed that his life would not be safe should he return to Birmingham, and

[1] Langford, i. 497.   [2] Ibid. i. 499.   [3] Field, *Life of Parr*, i. 309.
[4] Rutt, ii. 119.

that the dominant party would take no adequate precautions. So the sermon was read by another to the joint congregations of the Old and New Meetings.

Priestley followed up his sermon with an *Appeal to the Public on the Subject of the Riots in Birmingham*. Naturally enough he felt bitter at having his home broken up and his life endangered; and he was firmly of opinion that all this could have been prevented had the magistrates acted promptly. Before its publication he sent copies to Wedgwood, Keir, and other of his Birmingham friends; both Keir and Wedgwood thought it might be softened in part, Wedgwood disapproving of Priestley's bitterness.[1]

When Priestley was certain that he could not return to Birmingham he settled at Clapton. Soon he was asked to fill the position of minister at the New Gravel Pit Chapel at Hackney, which had been vacated by the death of Dr. Price. He also occupied himself with giving lectures on Natural Philosophy at the Dissenting college at Hackney. He was happy in his proximity to the Lindseys and other Dissenting friends. Sometimes he attended Whig parties, and he mentioned dining with Sheridan, where Fox had been expected but had not come. Samuel Rogers met him several times and was touched by his charm. He recounted that when an offensive visitor asked him how many books he had written, Priestley replied, 'Many more, Sir, than I should like to read'.[2]

Along with Wilberforce, Bentham, Sir Samuel Romilly, and others, Priestley had conferred upon him the honour of French citizenship. His answer to Burke was praised by the 'Society of the Friends of the Constitution, sitting at the Jacobins', in the letter of condolence they wrote Priestley after the riots. Now a fresh honour was

[1] Meteyard, ii. 605.   [2] Rogers, *Table Talk*, p. 124.

conferred upon him, for he was invited to sit in the National Assembly, but he declined.

'To the members of the National Assembly of France.

'Gentlemen,

'I have just received a notice by M. François of my being made a citizen of France, and also of my nomination, by the department of the Orne, to your approaching National Convention. Both of them I consider as the greatest of honours. At the same time, by conferring them on foreigners (tho', in my case, you have been led to over-rate the merit of an individual), you show a generous disposition to associate all the nations in the common cause of liberty, and the rights of men.

'The honour of *citizenship* with you I gratefully accept for myself, as I did for my son, and I trust we shall both of us endeavour to discharge the duty of good citizens of France, without violating any that are due to our native country, which from this time I trust will be united with you in the bonds of fraternal concord. But the more honourable appointment to your conventional Assembly I must decline, from a sense of my incapacity to discharge the duties of it to advantage, on account of my not being sufficiently acquainted with your language, and the particular circumstances of your country; and I should think it wrong to exclude another person better qualified on those respects.

'Presuming, however, from the choice that has been made of me, that some regard will be paid to my opinion, as far as that of a stranger may be competent, I shall not fail to give it hypothetically, with respect to some of the questions that I presume must come before the Assembly; and in some cases it is possible that a person at a distance may suggest useful hints to persons of better judgement, but whose passions may be too much agitated by the near view of interesting scenes. This I shall do in my correspondence with M. François, who is also chosen a member of the Convention, with leave to communicate my letters to the Assembly.

'Be assured that, tho' absent from you, my heart is with you; and you shall always command my best judgement, be it of ever so little value. I look upon your revolution as a new and most important era in the history of mankind. Yours is the honour of setting the great example; but the benefit to be derived from it will accrue not only to all Europe, but eventually to all the world.

'With the greatest respect and veneration,
I am, Gentlemen,
Your fellow citizen and humble servant,
J. PRIESTLEY.

Clapton, Jan le 13 1792. Year of liberty 4.'[1]

In 1793 war broke out between France and England. The British Government had already taken fright and was beginning its reign of persecution which culminated in the trial and acquittal of Horne Tooke, Hardy, Holcroft and others for High Treason in this country, and in Scotland in the condemnation and transportation of Fyshe-Palmer and Muir. In August, 1793, Priestley wrote that his friend Thomas Walker would be arrested should he appear in Manchester 'and sent literally in irons to Lancaster, with every insult'.[2] Winterbotham, a Dissenting minister, was found guilty of seditious expressions in two sermons 'on the evidence of two very illiterate

---

[1] From the original in the possession of the late Dr. Edgar Fahls Smith, of the University of Pennsylvania. Also see *Works*, xxv.   [2] Rutt, ii. 205.

persons, against the testimony of a great number of his respectable hearers, that he had not used any such language as was ascribed to him'.[1] If such was the fate of a minor Dissenting minister, no wonder that a more important one like Priestley believed that at any moment he might become the victim of a Government persecution. His sons found it difficult, if not impossible, to get employment at home. First emigration to France was considered and the French Government offered Priestley the use of a monastery near Toulouse; but when the sons decided to sail for America, Priestley and his wife concluded that the best and happiest thing they could do would be to follow them across the Atlantic. So on April 7th, 1794, after bidding farewell to their friends, whom they knew they would never see again, they embarked at Gravesend on the *Samson*.

[1] Rutt, ii. 206.

CHAPTER XI

THE VOYAGE ACROSS THE ATLANTIC
AND ARRIVAL IN AMERICA

THE voyage across the Atlantic took the Priestleys two
months and four days, not an excessive time in the
days before steam. More fortunate than their friends the
Russells, their voyage was unmolested by English or
French ships of war or privateers. Mrs. Priestley wrote
home that at times the voyage had been unpleasant from
the roughness of the weather, 'but as variety is charming,
we had all that well could be experienced on board, but
shipwreck and famine'. They passed 'mountains of ice,
larger than the Captain had ever seen before'. At another
time they saw 'water spouts great part of the day' which
happily 'kept at a proper distance', and they experienced
'billows mountain high'. One day a gale caught the ship
in full sail and carried away the top sails but, wrote the
intrepid Mrs. Priestley, 'I found myself more vexed than
frightened, and I fancy it might have been much lessened
by care'. Poor Mrs. Priestley suffered much more from
sickness than she had expected and spent the first three
weeks in bed. After that she recovered, and for the last
few days before land was sighted she was as well as ever
she was in her life. From her experience she advised
subsequent voyagers to lay in stores of those things they
could not bear on land.

'As to mental provision, I would wish everyone to lay
in a large store. Mine sufficed for myself, but I had not
the power to distribute it in the same manner as the
eatables I took. I would recommend everyone to have
motives strong enough to overbalance every inconvenience they meet with on the voyage. I would
also advise them to lay in a great stock of patience;

and where so many are to be so long together in so small a compass, they should make up their minds to bear and forbear; and I should think for their own happiness, they would wish to consult the good of those about them, which would make them feel their own grievances less. I was hurt to see in general that none troubled themselves about the sufferings of others.' [1]

The Doctor fared better than his wife and was less troubled with sickness. The ship, he said, was excellent, 'but the Captain not the man he had been represented to me. He swore much, and was given to liquor, and the crew very disorderly.' He was generous and good-natured and treated the Priestleys well, but owing to an unfortunate quarrel between Captain and Mate, no proper care was taken of the water casks, resulting in suffering among the steerage passengers, 'and if the voyage had been longer, the consequences might have been serious'. [2] The cooking was so bad, and it took more than half the voyage before Priestley had any appetite at all. He became so reconciled to the sea that he would have willingly gone round the world. [3] The cabin passengers proved agreeable, though aristocratically inclined. There was more religion among the steerage passengers than in the cabin. Though universally Calvinists they were tolerant enough to ask Priestley to perform divine service, a request which gave great pleasure and which he did when the 'weather and other circumstances would permit'. [3]

Writing on board was difficult, Priestley found long-hand particularly troublesome, but he wrote enough to make two sermons on the causes of infidelity. He had his favourite books with him, and read the whole of the Greek

[1] Rutt, ii. 235–6.   [2] Ibid. ii. 244.   [3] Ibid. ii. 259.

Testament, and the Hebrew Bible as far as the first book
of Samuel, and the second volume of Hartley. 'For
amusement', he had, 'several books of voyages and Ovid's
"Metamorphoses".'[1] Buchanan's poems, Petrarch's 'De
remediis', Erasmus's 'Dialogues', and Peter Pindar's
poems, the last of which pleased him more than he expected, provided mere light reading. He tried the heat
of the water at various depths, 'made other observations,
which suggest various experiments'.[2]

Sandy Hook was reached on June 1st, but the Priestleys
did not arrive at New York until the 4th. They landed at
the Battery and went to a house near-by which had been
the head-quarters of Howe and Clinton during the
Revolution. Young Joseph and his wife had been
awaiting them for some days, and they had already experienced some of the bigotry that was to meet Priestley.
On the first day of June they attended the new Presbyterian meeting where Dr. Rodgers was preaching.
Afterwards he administered 'The Lord's Supper to near
two hundred people, who, in companies of forty or fifty
at a time, succeeded each other in a large enclosed part of
the Meeting, near the communion table. "I invite", says
he, "all of you to partake of the Lord's Supper; but none",
said he, lifting up his hand and throwing his palm outward towards Governor Clinton's seat, where the
Priestleys were, "no, none of those who deny the Divinity
of our Saviour".'[3]

A traveller through the States at that time had compared
the principal cities with those of England. 'Boston', he
wrote, 'is the Bristol, New York the Liverpool, and
Philadelphia the London.' No other place which Priestley visited can have undergone a change anything like as
great as New York, but one point the town of 33,000

---

[1] Ibid. ii. 245.   [2] Ibid. ii. 245.   [3] Wansey, 71.

inhabitants shared with the largest city of to-day—'House rent is very dear.'

No sooner had they heard news of Priestley's arrival than most of the principal people came to call upon him, and first among these were Governor Clinton, and Dr. Prevoost, Bishop of New York. The bigotry of the clergy prevented Priestley receiving invitations to occupy their pulpits, but it did not stand in the way of friendship. Perhaps, as Priestley expressed it, they looked upon him with dread.[1] A fortnight later, on Trinity Sunday, the clergyman of the place generally improved the occasion by preaching for the Trinity, and Dr. Abraham Beach[2] seized the opportunity of preaching against Priestley. That stalwart episcopal clergyman, who is reported to have prayed for his King, as long as it was safe, took for his text 'Acquaint thou thyself with God, and be at peace with Him, thereby good shall come unto thee'. 'In a very personal manner, he applied them to Dr. Priestley, as if the cause of all his troubles was his ignorance of the nature of the Deity.'[3]

Priestley was enchanted with the prospects of America. He had never seen a place he liked so well as New York.[4] After a fortnight there, he wrote to Lindsey that should he, too, wish to emigrate he would come back and fetch him. He was delighted with the sense of perfect security and liberty. No beggars were to be seen anywhere, 'and whether it be the effect of general liberty, or some other cause,' Priestley declared that there were many more clever men than he had met anywhere in England.[5]

Addresses of welcome were presented by all the leading New York Societies. The Democratic and the Tammany

[1] Rutt, ii. 256.
[2] Abraham Beach is great-great-grandfather to the author. There are many family traditions regarding his exploits in the Revolution.
[3] Wansey, p. 191.   [4] Rutt, ii. 246.   [5] Ibid. ii. 256.

Society sent formal addresses of welcome, so did the 'Associated Teachers', the Medical Society, and the 'Republican Natives of Great Britain and Ireland'. The address of the last of these declared that finding opposition to tyranny useless many of its members had been forced to find shelter in America. They were happy in the blessings of the Government and only lamented the existence of slavery. In his reply Priestley merely noted the superiority of republican over monarchical forms of government, and though not holding everything American perfect, believed it would prove easier to reform abuses in the New World than in the Old. He did not see that in this case it would cost a civil war.

Replying to the Democratic Society Priestley declared that, while he hoped to find better security from violence in America than he had in England, he could not be a better subject. Though he might complain of the unjust treatment he had met with in England, he wished her prosperity. It was his hope that all former animosities between the two countries should be forgotten and that perpetual friendship should exist between them.[1]

Priestley was much gratified with the attention and friendliness shown him. He dined with General Gates, the veteran, if not always admirable, general of the Revolutionary War. At a large party at Mr. Osgood's, Wansey found himself placed between the Doctor and the Bishop of New York. 'I could not help remarking', he wrote, 'that I was seated between the Bishop and Dr. Priestley, the seat of war in England, but of peace and civility here.'[2]

On June 18th the Priestleys left New York for Philadelphia, at that time the capital of the States. The Quaker City was famous for its wealth and luxury, and it has been

---

[1] Rutt, ii. 248.   [2] Wansey, p. 189.

suggested that Priestley's dislike of the city was due to the vulgar ostentation of the rich Quakers, who displayed gold-headed canes and snuff-boxes.[1] As in New York, the rents were high, and prohibitive to one whose income went by English standards. The cost of living was so great that Priestley early discovered he could not support his family without making greater efforts than would be congenial at his time of life. There were no amenities except for the square adjoining the State House[2] (now Independence Hall). It was only a place for business, and to make money in. In addition, the summer climate of Philadelphia, even now dreaded, was then dangerous. The yellow fever had raged here during the preceding year, and in 1798 reduced the city almost to a wilderness. Though he might prefer New York to Philadelphia, Priestley realized that greater opportunities awaited him here.

Franklin had founded the American Philosophical Society, and Philadelphia undoubtedly was the centre of learning and science. He was welcomed by Benjamin Rush, who had learnt medicine at Edinburgh, and had been a representative in the Congress that signed the Declaration of Independence. He was as well known as a philanthropist as a politician, and was an early worker in the field of abolition of slavery. During the yellow fever he had proved his intrepidity as a physician, but his method of dealing with the disease by blood-letting aroused controversy. Priestley later believed him to be a Unitarian, but we gather he did not often put in an attendance at Priestley's services. There was also Dr. James Logan, a Quaker, who, when the continuance of peace between the United States and France lay in the balance, proceeded on a private peace expedition. Priestley had already exchanged letters with Dr. Abercrombie,

---

[1] Ernest Fahls Smith, *Priestley in America*.　　[2] Rutt, ii. 269.

an eloquent and learned clergyman of the Episcopal Church. John Vaughan, a son of his old friend Samuel and brother of Benjamin, was settled in Philadelphia and took charge of the Priestleys. Vaughan lived to a good old age, and was noted for his kindliness to those in distress. Half a century later, when Louis Philippe was forced to abdicate, Philadelphia is said to have hourly expected to see the French King walking down Front Street or Market Street on the arm of John Vaughan.[1]

Priestley found his welcome gratifying. The members of the American Philosophical Society, to which he belonged, hastened to send their congratulations on the arrival of their distinguished member. But the friendship of learned societies could not make up for disappointment in there being offered no pulpit. 'Nobody asks me to preach', he wrote home, 'and I hear there is much jealousy and dread of me.'[2] But Priestley perceived signs favourable to the spread of Unitarianism, and he set about printing some of his works. The Universalists were building themselves a church and, more liberal than Christians usually are, meant to open it to any sect of Christians three days a week. Priestley's friends hoped that, by their contributing towards the expense of building it, he would be allowed the use of it on Sunday mornings, a hope which was fulfilled the following year.

The original intention of the Priestleys had been to settle with their sons on the Susquehanna. Thomas Cooper, Vaughan, Priestley, and others had contracted for 100,000 acres, but Cooper's absence in England had led to disagreement and the scheme was given up. But it had not been finally renounced when the Priestleys decided to leave Philadelphia and set out on the long and difficult journey to the small Pennsylvanian town of Northumberland.

---

[1] Furness, *Sermon.*   [2] Rutt, ii. 263.

CHAPTER XII

LAST YEARS
1794–1800

THE traveller to-day who covers the one hundred and thirty odd miles from Philadelphia to Northumberland can little realize what the journey was like in the last decade of the eighteenth century. Not only was it the period before steam, but for that district the period before stage-coaches, and before bridges were general. Five days were spent on the road, where hours now suffice, travelling in whatsoever manner of cart could be got. Priestley and his wife were prepared for hardships, but the journey turned out worse than they had expected. The summer rains had already delayed their departure from Philadelphia, but even when they set out 'the creeks were so swelled with the rains', the Doctor wrote to Vaughan, 'that it was with great difficulty the waggon loaded with stores, got over, we and the baggage were ferried over in a canoe. Had we not been stopped by a friendly countryman, who saw us at a distance, our driver would have driven in, and we should all have perished.'¹ Not only was the journey rough and dangerous but the inns were frightful. According to a contemporary description three beds in a room were usual, and these were generally infested by bugs. At Harrisburgh Priestley hired 'a common waggon' in which he and his wife 'slept the two last nights, being much more comfortable than in the inns'.

But the journey at last came to an end, and Northumberland, lying among the Alleghanies at the point where the northern and western branches of the Susquehanna meet, must have seemed a haven and a quiet resting-place to the travellers after the turmoil and anxiety of the past few

¹ *Pa. Hist. Soc. MSS.*

years. Still it was a long way from civilization, far from scholarly neighbours, almost the end of the world. Except for the store of a French trader the place had been uninhabited until 1760, when a man named Martin erected a house there and opened a tavern. The town was laid out twelve years later, but had been abandoned during the revolutionary wars when the Indians regained possession. With the restoration of peace the white settler returned, and by 1794 the town numbered a hundred houses. Next year the Post Office was opened.

The young Priestleys and Thomas Cooper were still considering the possibilities of a settlement further inland, where there might be gathered together all those immigrants who had suffered in the Old World from the intolerance and prejudice of their neighbours. Northumberland was not looked on first of all as a final destination. Priestley did not expect to spend his remaining years in retirement, but believed he was called on to be the Apostle of Rational Religion in the New World, and for such activity Northumberland would be no centre. In fact, in his first letter to John Vaughan, Priestley's thought was that it would be no place at all to live in. He would return and settle in the outskirts of Philadelphia (perhaps Germantown would be the place for him), 'therefore I hope you are looking out for a proper house for me, though my wife thinks we shall not fix upon anything till the Spring.'

But Priestley quickly gave up all thought of settling in Philadelphia, and was horrified when Vaughan wrote that he had found a house for him. Mrs. Priestley had taken 'an unconquerable aversion to Philadelphia, and my evil genius', he wrote, 'having brought her hither, I must give her the choice of a place of residence'.[1] Northumberland

---

[1] Northumberland, Aug. 12th, 1794. From copy of letter in possession of Mrs. Belloc-Lowndes.

would suit him very well, 'and if I get my books and instruments hither, I think I can be both as happy and useful, as anywhere else, tho' many things will still be wanting to me. I shall spend some part of the winter, or spring with you.'[1] Mrs. Priestley was delighted with Northumberland.[2]

'I am happy and thankful,' she wrote, 'to meet with so sweet a situation and so peaceful a retreat as the place I now write from. Dr. Priestley also likes it and of his own choice intends to settle here, which is more than I hoped for at the time we came up. . . . This country is very delightful, the prospects of wood and water more beautiful than I have ever seen before, the people plain and decent in their manners.'

By the end of August Priestley had chosen a site, overlooking the Susquehanna, on which to build his house. 'I do not think', he wrote to Belsham, 'there can be, in any part of the world, a more delightful situation than this, and the neighbourhood and the conveniences of the place are improving daily.' All that was needed was congenial society, and if only Belsham himself and Mr. and Mrs. Lindsey would come all would be well. 'We could take our walks along the banks of the Susquehanna, and ramble as I often do, in the woods, as we used to do about Hackney. Here we should have no apprehension of powder sugar being mistaken for gunpowder, or metaphorical gunpowder for real.'[3]

House building then was not the rapid process it has now become in the United States. Of whatever the house was built the material had first of all to be prepared. Owing to the wet and unhealthy summer it was impossible to bake bricks, and as there was no seasoned wood at

[1] Northumberland, Aug. 12th, 1794. From copy of letter in possession of Mrs. Belloc-Lowndes.   [2] *Collection of Letters.*   [3] Rutt, ii. 270, 272.

hand, the timber for a house had first of all to be dried. This was done in the following manner.

'To kiln-dry boards we dig a trench about two feet deep, the length of the boards and what breadth you please. We then support the boards with the edges downwards, and so that when the fire is made under them, the smoke and heat may have access to every part of them. Two or three stages are placed one over another, and, on the outside, boards to keep off the rain. In ten days they will be as much dried as by exposure to the air two years. We commonly kiln-dry ten thousand feet at a time. The firewood must be such as is not apt to flame, lest the boards should take fire, which sometimes happens. The expense cannot be much. A house constructed with such boards I prefer to one of brick and stone.' [1]

Skilled labour was scarce, and Priestley had difficulty in finding the necessary carpenters. In October, 1794, writing to Dr. Benjamin Rush, at Philadelphia, he asked whether he could send carpenters.[2] The house is still standing, and may be visited by any one who journeys to Northumberland. Unfortunately railway lines have been built on both sides of it. It is comfortably planned and is well proportioned. It is less its simplicity of construction than the elaborateness of design which is surprising when one bears in mind how much Northumberland was then in the backwoods.

During the first autumn, Priestley was invited to fill the chair of chemistry in the University of Pennsylvania. If the invitation had come earlier, before he had settled at Northumberland, he would most likely have accepted. As it was he hesitated for some time before refusing. It

---

[1] *Scientific Correspondence*, pp. 154, 155.   [2] Ibid. 142.

was not only the professorship which almost lured him back to Philadelphia, but the desire nearest to his heart, of founding there a Unitarian congregation.[1] But he had already gone to considerable expense in moving his library, apparatus, and other possessions to Northumberland, and the pleasanter climate, and comparative low cost of living led to his refusal. Priestley was also anxious to found a college at Northumberland, but after several persons had interested themselves in it, the scheme was finally dropped. If it had taken shape Priestley hoped it would give impetus to the founding of a Unitarian congregation. The meeting houses were closed to him and he had to satisfy himself with reading a sermon in his own house or at his son's.[2] 'His discourses', wrote one of his small congregation of this period, 'were usually practical, easy to be understood, reducible to common life. In his prayers he was devout, free from the error which many fall into of multiplying words, when addressing the Divine Being, as though he wanted information.'[3] His service to Unitarianism was rather indirect. 'As to Unitarianism, it is, I perceive', he wrote to Lindsey, 'greatly promoted by my coming hither, and the circulation of my publications, and probably in a more effectual way than it would have been done by my acting more openly.'[4] He looked forward to visiting Philadelphia annually for the special purpose of preaching there, appearing in his proper character as minister of the gospel, and giving series of lectures on the Evidences of the Christian Religion.

Meanwhile the first winter passed. The Doctor gave up his wig, since in such an out of the way spot no one could be found to dress it, and in all his later portraits he is

---

[1] *Scientific Correspondence*, pp. 144, 145.   [2] Rutt, ii. 284.
[3] *Monthly Repository*, i. 394–5; Rutt, ii. 281.   [4] Rutt, ii. 281.

depicted wearing his own hair. But what was worse than giving up the wig, which, after all, was very likely an advantage, he began to lose his front teeth, and this he believed to be a sign that the last change would not be far off, nor could he consider it undesirable. 'Then my present state of exile, for so I consider it, from all that I hold dear, will be over.' [1]

During this winter he was at work on his Church History. Experiments he found difficult, for as yet he had no proper laboratory, and his instruments and books were all in one room at his son's house. The rise in the cost of living was worrying, but soon Priestley hoped to be independent, as his sons would raise all that they needed. 'Even I', he wrote to Lindsey, 'sometimes take my axe or my mattock and work, as long as I can, along with them. Nobody here thinks himself above bodily labour of any kind, and they dress accordingly.' [2] His youngest son was taking to farming as a duck to water, and his proud father remarked, 'Harry will make a spirited and laborious farmer. He is the wonder of the place, and, I hope, will not fail to do well.' [3]

With the exception of Thomas Cooper, Priestley had very little congenial society at Northumberland, even if that can be called congenial, since the two of them differed on religion. Priestley had hoped that Benjamin Vaughan, who, after his active sympathies with the French Revolutionists, considered a return to England unwise, would join some of his brothers in America, and settle at Philadelphia. But Vaughan seems to have considered the friendship undesirable, and settled in New England. From an observation in a later letter of Priestley's to John Vaughan, we gather that Benjamin, not having his brother's kindness, even found the

---

[1] Ibid. 292.   [2] Ibid. ii. 301.   [3] Ibid. ii. 304.

correspondence with the Doctor embarrassing, and that John had been given the disagreeable task of hinting that it should cease. And in a letter of Adams [1] to Pickering it is clear that when Benjamin called on the then Vice-President at Quincy he took care to dissociate himself from the acts and principles of his old teacher.

In the summer Priestley was cheered by a visit from his old friends, and fellow-sufferers, the Russells. Like him they had determined to emigrate, leaving behind the tyrannous government of England for the greater freedom of America. But fortune had favoured them less than it had Priestley, and the American ship on which they sailed was captured by the French frigate, *Proserpine*; though the ship was allowed to go on its voyage, the Russells were removed to the French vessel and for five months they were imprisoned on different ships at Brest. After liberation they spent about six months in Paris, becoming more critical of the French Revolution, and then proceeded to New York. In September, much to Priestley's delight, they visited him at Northumberland.

'My prospect is much improved by the arrival of Mr. Russell and his family, who are now with us, and seem to like the place so well as to settle in it. He has, however, taken a house in Philadelphia, where he will reside in the winter, and where it is settled that I am to be his guest, as long as I choose to continue there, which will add much to my satisfaction.' [2]

But the young Russells did not care for Northumberland and decided to settle in Connecticut.

Before Priestley's visit that winter to Philadelphia, the first sorrow of his American life overtook him. This was the death of his youngest and favourite son, Harry.

---

[1] Adams, *Works,* ix. 13.   [2] Rutt, ii. 317.

His father had been so proud of his skill and energy as a farmer, but it is supposed that the young man overtaxed his strength. It was the first personal loss that Priestley had experienced. Of all his children, he thought him the most like what he was at the same age and had the greatest hopes of him.

It had all along been Priestley's intention to spend two months of every year in Philadelphia. 'But one thing is necessary to this', he had written to John Vaughan, 'and I shall with great freedom mention it to you. My desire, and I think my duty, is to appear in my proper character of a Minister of the Gospel, and I will not make any considerable stay in your city, and be reduced to a disgraceful silence by the bigotry and jealousy of the preachers.'[1] Vaughan was to discuss the project with their mutual friends, but if Philadelphia would have none of him Priestley intended to try New York.

In February, Priestley, accompanied by his daughter-in-law, set out for Philadelphia on a visit to the Russells. Mrs. Priestley's dislike of American towns was invincible, and she stayed behind. There were her other sons, and grandchildren to be cared for. How far the visit was agreeable to the rest of the family is conjecture, but young Thomas did not like his father's guest.

'Dr. Priestley', he wrote, 'is undoubtedly a very virtuous, learned, and agreeable man, and his name will be handed down to posterity as a great philosopher, and as one who dared to reduce religion to the laws of reason and common sense by chasing the superstitions and prejudices that had till then veiled not only the Catholic but Protestant faith, yet he is not one with whom one could enjoy the pleasures of domestic

[1] *Belloc-Lowndes MSS.*

O

intercourse. In the little occurrences of a family he is apt to be discontented and fretful. In case everything does not go to his mind, he will be upon the fidgets until it is rectified, and perhaps for some time after. In short he displays a degree of selfishness which I should never have suspected from one who acts so disinterestedly in greater things. But who can lay a just claim to the title of a consistent character through all events and circumstances?' [1]

Priestley now set out to fulfil his purpose of preaching and delivering a set of discourses on the Evidences of Christianity. On February 14th having 'the use of Mr. Winchester's pulpit', the Universalist Church which was now built, Priestley preached his 'first sermon to a very numerous, respectable, and very attentive audience'. George Thatcher, who attended, wrote immediately to Dr. Freeman of Boston, 'I have just returned from the Universalist meeting house and I hasten to tell you I had the pleasure of hearing our friend Dr. Priestley'. Priestley had preached to a crowded congregation. 'He gave universal satisfaction, for as I returned in the street it seemed as if every tongue was engaged in speaking his praise, or answering the clergy of the City.' Five years earlier a preacher 'who called himself a Unitarian, gave out that on a certain day he should deny and publicly disprove the Calvinistic idea of the Divinity of Jesus, in consequence of which declaration the room, which the preacher had engaged by contract for two or three months, was taken from him, and the door nailed up, and he was obliged to flee from the City. But now such a preacher is listened to with pleasing attention, and attended by a thronging multitude.' [2] Among those whom Thatcher

---

[1] *Russells of Birmingham*, pp. 206–7.
[2] *Mass. Hist. Soc. Transactions*, 2nd Series, vol. iii.

noted were 'The Vice-President, Elsworth, Cabot, Sedg-
wick, and many others, of both Houses of Congress.
Judge Preble, with whom I spoke after service, expressed
himself in raptures—"Good God", said he, "what would
I give to hear him as long as I live?".'[1] A listener on the
following Sunday, noted 'the deep attention of a very
numerous audience'.[2] Priestley found the congregation
numerous and respectable, and determined to dedicate
the discourses to John Adams, the Vice-President, since
he was 'most punctual in his attendance, and an old
acquaintance and correspondent'.[3] There was hope of
forming a Society of Unitarians. 'There is really a noble
harvest here. We want nothing but able labourers.'[3]
If there was no chance of a trained minister his place could
be taken by laymen; and for nearly thirty years the services of this society, founded with the encouragement of
Priestley, were conducted by John Vaughan, who 'read
printed discourses', Mr. Taylor, and Mr. Eddowes, who
composed their own sermons.[4] Priestley wondered if
there was a chance of obtaining a minister from England.
He wrote to Kenrick of Exeter that he of all persons
would be the most proper for the undertaking, but,

'Philadelphia is a place above measure expensive, and
living there is to me very irksome, especially in
summer, and must be so to every one who has English
habits and whose most intimate friends must be left
behind him in England. On this account a young man,
of some fortune, and few connexions, would be the
most proper. But where shall we find such a man, of
sufficient zeal, and other necessary qualifications; and
we see that few young men can be depended upon.'[5]

The change from Northumberland to Philadelphia was

[1] Ibid.   [2] *Mass. Hist. Soc. MSS.*   [3] Rutt, ii. 336.
[4] Furness, *Sermon.*   [5] Copy in *Dr. Williams' Library,* Oct. 28th, 1796.

indeed pleasant. On his arrival at William Russell's, Priestley had found his host 'engaged to drink tea with the President, where we accompanied him, and spent two hours as in any private family. He invited me to come at any time, without any ceremony.' Adams, the Vice-President was still his friend. Priestley found life leisurely, and amused himself by attending debates in the House of Representatives which, he declared, compared very favourably with the House of Commons. 'A Mr. Amos speaks as well as Mr. Burke; but, in general, the speakers are more argumentative, and less rhetorical. And whereas there are not with you more than ten or a dozen tolerable speakers, here every member is capable of speaking, which makes interesting debates tedious.'[1]

It is recounted that Priestley was a charming talker, whatever may have been his foibles as a writer. One story is told how, when calling at a friend's house, a confirmed Calvinist came in, and seated himself next to him and enjoyed a charming conversation. When Priestley left, he asked his host, 'Who is that delightful old gentleman I have been conversing with?' for he had not heard his name. On hearing who it was the Calvinist replied, 'All that I have formerly said respecting Dr. Priestley is nonsense. I have now seen him for myself, and remember, I will never forgive you if you do not put me in the way of seeing more of him.'[2] The following year another visitor to Philadelphia wrote,

'I found Dr. Priestley had been well received in the city by many, though there were some minds in which prejudice ran very high. One gentleman told me he thought the Doctor did not put on respectability enough, but made himself familiar with the lower

1 Rutt, ii. 340.   2 Ibid. ii. 343.

orders, and had preached a discourse for the benefit of the Emigrant Society; and that one of the public papers was engaged against him.'[1]

At the end of May Priestley returned to Northumberland. He hoped that shortly his house would be habitable. His wife had taken great trouble in its internal planning, but in September she was taken ill. The anxieties of the last few years, as well as the loss of her favourite son, had told on even her heroic self. On September 11th she died 'in the 55th year of her age'. She was buried beside her son in the Friends' Graveyard and on her tomb Priestley had engraved:

'God shall wipe away all tears from their eyes and there shall be no more death, neither shall there be any more pain: for the former things are passed away.'

It was Priestley's faith which alone saved him from being inconsolable. Never in adversity did his trust in the Divine goodness weaken, yet, as he wrote to Lindsey, 'I never stood in more need of friendship than I do now'. The house was almost ready 'and promises to be everything she had wished. . . . For activity in continuing and executing everything usually done by women, and some things done by men, I do not think she ever had a superior, or in generosity and disinterestedness; always caring for others, and never for herself.'[2] To distract his thoughts Priestley considered the possibilities of a missionary tour through parts of the continent—a plan which was not realized.[3] Until his house was ready he went to live with his son Joseph, whom he intended to bring back with him as he could not undertake housekeeping. His desire was to die and be buried near his wife, though he hoped to visit England once more.

[1] *Monthly Repository* i. 1806.   [2] Rutt, ii. 354.   [3] Ibid. ii. 355.

That winter Priestley was again in Philadelphia. He had been suggested as a possible alternative to Jefferson as President of the Philosophical Society, 'but I gave my informant', wrote Priestley, 'good reason why they should not make choice of me',[1] and Jefferson was duly chosen. He found the Unitarian Society flourishing, though without a minister. 'The service is read with great propriety and seriousness, by persons appointed by ballot. I have been here only one Sunday, and Dr. Price's sermon on the Resurrection of Lazarus was read. Each reader selects and composes his prayers as he pleases; and they do not in general prefer a Liturgy.'[2]

His first discourse this winter was attended by Mr. Liston, the English Ambassador. Priestley dined with him and found him 'a pleasing, liberal man'. His predecessor, George Hammond, the first British Minister to the United States, Priestley believed, had 'patronised the writer of that scurrilous pamphlet relating to my emigration'.[3]

Priestley went to bid farewell to Washington, of whose last presidency he did not always approve, and was invited to Mount Vernon, an invitation of which he never availed himself. Of the new President he hoped better things, and had no forebodings that Adams's term of office would prove one of personal vexation. Jefferson, now Vice-President, he saw frequently and noticed him among his congregation. 'I hope', wrote the preacher, 'that he is not an unbeliever, as he has been represented.'

When Priestley returned to his home in Northumberland, his laboratory was ready and he set to work to prove beyond all doubt his treasured theory of phlogiston.

---

[1] Rutt, ii. 362.   [2] Ibid. ii. 369.
[3] William Cobbett, who had emigrated to Philadelphia in 1792, had attacked Priestley in *Observations on Priestley's Emigration*.

By June he was sending to the press a pamphlet 'containing an answer to everything that I have seen in reply to my former'. He realized that his theory was not acceptable and that his character as a philosopher was suffering, 'but depend upon it, everything will be cleared up, and then I hope my character, as a theologian will gain in consequence of it; and it is in this light chiefly that I regard it. How insignificant are all subjects, compared to those which relate to religion!'[1]

Yellow fever was rampant in Philadelphia during the summer. Either on account of the ravages of the disease, or owing to the Alien and Sedition laws, the outcome of violent anti-French feeling, Priestley did not visit here again until 1801.

The difficulties and animosities left by the Treaty of Paris were brought to an end by Jay's Treaty, which, negotiated in 1798, was ratified in the following year. French fury know no bounds. The policy of issuing blank letters of marque, and of seizing every American ship on whatsoever excuse possible, was carried on with vigour. Neutrality seemed a word beyond the comprehension of French rulers. Their earlier policy, when Genet, brother of Madame Campan and 'quaintest of the many curious diplomats sent by European Governments to the United States'[2] had represented them, was to treat America as a dependent ally. Jefferson, friend to France though he was, had lectured this citizen of France on the law of Nations, quoting Vattel and Grotius.[3] His recall was demanded, but 'instead of returning to feed the guillotine, Genet married the daughter of Governor Clinton and settled down to the life of a country gentleman on the Hudson'.[4] We catch a glimpse of him, as a

<hr/>

[1] Ibid. ii. 381, 382.   [2] Morison, i. 150.
[3] Ibid. i. 153.   [4] Ibid. i. 154.

private individual, frequenting the same society in New York as did Priestley.

It was this hostility, and the refusal of the Directory to receive Monroe's successor as American Minister, which led to the dispatch of Elbridge Gerry, Pinckney and John Marshall to negotiate peace. Talleyrand, then foreign minister, began the negotiations by sending messengers, referred to in dispatches as *X*, *Y*, and *Z*, to ask, in the first place, a bribe for the minister and a loan. The Americans refused, but wrote home their experience, and the dispatches were published.[1] American opinion was justly incensed, but was wrong in believing that Talleyrand would save his face by engineering a declaration of war. Perhaps one advantage that the completely shameless has over the rest of the world, is that he has no pride to interfere with common sense. America waited for war. Alien and Sedition Acts were passed. Some Frenchmen, like Volney, thought it wise to leave America voluntarily before deportation should be the order of the day. Anti-French feeling ran high; those who like Priestley had sympathized at an earlier day with France, now believed they lay at the mercy of the 'American Reign of Terror'.

During these last years Priestley took no active part in public affairs, but it was impossible for one with his long connexion with English politics, and his sufferings, not to remain interested both in the general political situation of Europe and the domestic life of the United States. On arrival Priestley had been greeted as a martyr in freedom's cause. During his first visits to Philadelphia he was, as has been seen, an occasional visitor of the President, George Washington, and Adams had at one time been a member of his congregation, though it is true that as the time approached nearer his presidential election

[1] Morison, i. 208–9.

he ceased to attend. In the case of anti-French feeling, it was not remembered that they, who like Priestley had sympathized with the objects of the French Revolution had supported the American, and had done what little they could to prevent hostilities, and during the war had succoured American prisoners. Until he came under the stigma of the Alien Act, Priestley never clearly grasped that America and England were two distinct nations. Till then America was the England, on a large and predominant scale, of Lansdowne House and the philosophers of Birmingham, and the Americans were their countrymen. Priestley did not consciously try to take part in American politics. If that had been his desire he would not have settled at Northumberland, five days journey from Philadelphia with but one post a week. It would be easier to-day to carry on an English election campaign from New York. But he wished to propagate rational religion and he took part in celebrations connected with the revolution and wrote occasional letters on politics. No doubt it was unfortunate that Stone's very hostile letter from Paris, expressing his belief that before long England would be revolutionized with French aid, was intercepted, but it was scarcely fair that Priestley should be held responsible for the opinions of his correspondents. Priestley in his defence, admitted his belief that a more radical revolution was now necessary than a mere reformation of abuses in English government, but he wished it to be 'effected peaceably, and without the interference of any foreign power'.[1] Priestley defined Revolution in the terms of 1688, not of 1798.

Some of his friends, Lindsey in particular, disapproved of his *Letters to the Inhabitants of Northumberland*.[2] John Vaughan seems to have made a journey to North-

---

[1] *Works*, xxv. 131. [2] Ibid. xxv.

umberland on purpose to persuade Priestley to refrain from publishing.

'Your account of our friend surprises me, notwithstanding what I have known of him,' wrote Benjamin to John, 'I do not wonder that he cannot comprehend our motives on these delicate subjects, for I never could comprehend his. I cannot conceive, however, that he will be meddled with here, except in newspapers: but if he will deal in print himself, he must bear to be attacked in print. Happy indeed would it have been for him, had he lived near us, instead of near his present fiery friends.'[1]

One of Priestley's opponents, Nicholas Ridgeby, expressed a desire to see these letters and added 'This eldest Son of Disorder will never obtain his sought-for "Repose" on this side of the Grave; and I believe the Government of Heaven itself, should he ever get there, will, in his opinion, want reformation'.[2]

The Letters were originally published in 1799, and a second edition appeared in 1801. In them Priestley defended himself and gave an account of his principles, political and religious. George Thatcher, a federalist, but all the same a friend of Priestley's, probably thought that Priestley's defence was unnecessary, for in a letter to him on December 12, 1799, Priestley said:

'The Porcupine's abuse had no effect on you, it had on many others; that even in this part of the country I was generally regarded as a dangerous person. For in this country it is not one person in a hundred that knows anything of my writings, or of my history. I was frequently called an *atheist*. Porcupine's paper was taken by all the most reputable federalists in these

[1] *Belloc-Lowndes MSS.*   [2] *Pa. Hist. Soc. MSS.*, Dec. 21st 1799.

parts, and many I believe propagated suspicion of me that they did not entertain themselves.'[1]

'For five years,' he declared in a subsequent letter, he had not meddled with politics; 'and yet no person in this country has been exposed to such outrageous abuse . . . The virulence of Porcupine is taken up by other writers, but I have mended myself a little here, and with that I am satisfied; and I hope I shall have no occasion to give you, or them, any further trouble in this way. It was with great reluctance that I did what I have done.'

Pickering, Adams's energetic Secretary of State, and perhaps even more energetic lieutenant to his unofficial chief, Alexander Hamilton, was anxious that the Alien Act should be put into force and an example made of Priestley.[2] This Act, luckily for the good fame of the young republic, remained a dead letter, and neither Priestley nor Cobbett nor any one else was deported. But it was possible under its provisions for the President on his own authority, without the victim knowing the charges against him, or having the power to make any defence, to order the deportation of any Alien. Fortunately for Priestley his former friend and member of his congregation had come to the conclusion that he was not worth the trouble. 'I do not think it wise', wrote Adams to Pickering, 'to execute the alien law against poor Priestley at present. He is as weak as water, as unstable as Rueben or the wind. His influence is not an atom in the world.'[3] But Priestley was warned that unless he was careful he might get into difficulties.

Priestley's friendship with Thomas Cooper was not conducive to tranquillity. Cooper had been a friend in

[1] *Mass. Hist. Soc. MSS.*   [2] Cf. Adams, *Works*, ix. 6.   [3] Ibid. ix. 14.

England in the peaceful days before the Revolution. His sympathy for French politics had not outlived a visit to Paris. 'I went over to France in 1792', he wrote, 'an enthusiast, I left in disgust.' He had preceded Priestley to America, on which occasion he had been armed with a letter of introduction from him to Adams. In 1795 he was naturalized, and while living in Priestley's house in Northumberland published *Political Essays*, for which in 1801 he was convicted for libel, under the Sedition Act, and sentenced to six months imprisonment and a fine. The fine was subsequently repaid his heirs. Jefferson declared him to be 'the greatest man in America, in powers of mind and in acquired information', and he rose to important positions in Pennsylvania and later in South Carolina.[1] A letter from Priestley recommending Cooper for some government post, which at the very worst was inexpedient, annoyed Adams considerably, and he believed Cooper's attack on his administration was the result of his neglect of the letter.[2]

The mistakes that the Federalists made amongst themselves, and the natural swing of the pendulum was bringing that peace and tranquillity which Priestley so much longed for, and Jefferson's election to the Presidency put his democrat friends in power. For some time he had known the new President and they liked each other. Jefferson regretted that Priestley had not settled in Virginia, rather than in Northumberland. 'You would have found there equal soil, the first climate, the most healthy air on earth, the homage of universal reverence and love, and the power of the country shed over you as a shield.'[3] The attacks of Porcupine and others shamed him, 'How deeply have I been chagrined and mortified,' he wrote,

---

[1] Malone, *Public Life of Cooper.*   [2] Adams, *Works*, ix. 13.
[3] Rutt, ii. 435, 436.

'at the persecution which fanaticism and monarchy have excited against you, even here!'

Precious indeed were these letters from Jefferson and a comfort to the unhappy old man in his disappointment. Copies were made of them and sent across the Atlantic to Lindsey. His friendship and correspondence during these last years were a continual source of happiness.

'To me the administration of Mr. Jefferson', wrote Priestley to Dr. Logan, 'is the cause of peculiar satisfaction, as I now, for the first time in my life (and I shall soon enter my 70th year) find myself in any degree of favour with the government of this country in which I have lived, and I hope I shall die in the same pleasing situation.'[1]

In his dedication of the volume of his Church History to Jefferson, he wrote:

'Having fled from a state of persecution in England, and having been not without cause of apprehension in the late administration here, I feel the greater satisfaction in the prospect of passing the remainder of an active life, when I naturally wish for repose, under your protection. Tho' I am arrived at the usual term of human life, it is now only that I can say I see nothing to fear from the hand of power, the government under which I live being for the first time truly favourable to me. And tho' I think it has been evident that I have never been improperly swayed by the mean principle of fear, it is certainly a happiness to be out of the possibility of its influence, especially towards the close of life; enjoying a degree of peace and rest, previous to the state of more perfect rest from labour in the grave; with the hope of rising to a state of greater

[1] *Pa. Hist. Soc. MSS.*

activity, security, and happiness beyond it. This is all that any man can wish, or have in this world; and this, Sir, under your administration I enjoy.'[1]

Priestley agreed with his friend, William Russell, that Jefferson's only possible rival in sphere of government was the Tsar Alexander,[2] who in 1801 inherited the crown of all the Russias. In this connexion we find Priestley, in a letter to Jefferson, asking that some one should draw up 'an account of the constitution of this country as my friend (Mr. Stone) says it will be agreeable to the Emperor, and I will transmit it to Mr. Stone'.[3]

The accusation which Cobbett levelled against Priestley was that of treason. Priestley was referred to in some such terms as the 'hoary old traitor'. But to any one who read his letters it is clear how unfair the accusation was. Priestley never cared for any country as well as his own. It was not hate, but love of it, which made him conscious of the imperfections of George III's régime. Not only had he suffered voluntary exile under the Pittite persecution, but he had seen his friends Muir and Fyshe-Palmer banished to Australia and abominably treated. In 1796, writing to Lindsey he observed, 'I feel as an Englishman, and shall sincerely lament any evil that may befall my native country, though I condemn as much as ever the conduct of its rulers'.[4] He undoubtedly expected to feel more at home in America than he did. He believed the American constitution to be the best yet devised by man. 'Without this persuasion I should not have come among you.'[5] Yet his admiration was not unqualified, and he shared with Jefferson the fear that the Presidency might become an office for life, a danger which was averted

[1] *Library of Congress MSS.*   [2] Rutt, ii. 474.
[3] Oct. 29th, 1802. *Library of Congress MSS.*
[4] Rutt, ii. 363.   [5] *Works*, xxv. 156.

through the good sense of the earlier Presidents. Priestley never became, and never intended to become naturalized.

Though the distance of America from Europe made news late, Priestley never lost interest in the affairs of the Old World. No doubt his interest was heightened by his belief that the prophecies of the Bible were about to be fulfilled. Not that his faith was altogether cheerful, for evil things were foretold. 'I cannot help fearing great calamity,' he wrote on the first day of 1798, 'as the prophecies announcing such, I think are about to be accomplished, or rather are accomplishing.'[1] Later he admitted that though the present state of things were wonderfully interesting it was 'to a Christian, full of consolation, though calamitous'.[2] 'The papal power, for the destruction of which we have so long prayed, is now fallen.' He read the news-sheets of the day with the Book of Daniel open before him. From Buonaparte's invasion of Egypt he expected great things to come, 'and those not intended by the French'.[3] He rejoiced at Nelson's success in the Battle of the Nile. It evidently 'encouraged', he wrote, 'the Turks, the Neapolitans, and Sardinians to declare against the French, and has hastened their downfall, for I hope that of the Turks is not far off, and this will be a glorious event indeed. Read the 19th chapter of Isaiah. Something favourable is promised to Egypt in the latter days, which is at hand, but I do not presume to say that Buonaparte is the *deliverer* there promised them. He may be cut off: but what is promised will no doubt be fulfilled.'[4] He hoped that the French keeping possession of Egypt, 'in which I rejoice', would end in the restoration of the Jews. It was a pleasant outlet from his own political worries to write to his friends on the prophecies.

[1] Rutt, ii. 390.   [2] Ibid. ii. 400.   [3] Ibid. ii. 410.   [4] Ibid. ii. 417.

'I wish,' he wrote to Dr. Rush, 'I could give you as much satisfaction with respect to the *prophecies* as you do to me with respect to *Medicine and Physiology*. The present time is certainly a most interesting one, and the fate of at least one of the monarchies of Europe, and especially that of the Pope, shews us where we are in the great chain of Events. I expect the downfall of all the states represented by the *ten toes* in the image of Nebuchadnezzar, and the *ten horns* of the 4th beast of Daniel before the present war be over. They were all to fall *together* and with *violence*. Egypt is, no doubt, to be raised from its late abject state about the same time, but whether by Buonaparte, or some other, we cannot presume to say. He may only be the *precursor* of their *great deliverer*. I think it more probable that the French nation will be the great instrument in the hands of God to effect these great things, as their leading men have no views of the kind; so that it will not be said hereafter that the prophecies have fulfilled themselves. I look for great things in the present generation. You are younger than I am, and will probably see them.'[1]

It seems as if Lindsey, who along with Belsham, Russell, and Dr. Rush were Priestley's confidants in his studies of the prophecies, did not altogether approve of Priestley's ideas concerning the Millennium, for in writing to Lindsey, Priestley says that his speculations about the Millennium and the present condition of Christ are innocent, but to himself they were 'something more than amusing'.[2] At the end of his letter to the inhabitants of Northumberland he drew attention to the scriptural promise of a nation 'now under the discipline of

---

[1] *Scientific Correspondence*, p. 156.   [2] Rutt, ii. 403.

Providence destined . . . to govern the world in peace, when *nation will no more rise up against nation* and when *they will learn war no more.*' The period of calamity, which should be marked by great destruction of men was verified by the condition of Europe. Belsham doubted the authority of Daniel, but Priestley's faith was firm. His critical abilities, so marked in the days of the *Theological Repository*, seem now to have weakened. He realized the danger of solitude; 'I find', he wrote, 'a great disadvantage in being *alone*, having no person whatever to confer with on any subject of this kind; and as we used to observe with respect to Mr. Cappe, my solitary speculations may lead me astray, farther than I can be aware of myself.'[1] The loss of Mrs. Priestley's common sense, and Lindsey's restraining power, was nowhere better illustrated than in these studies.

During these years of disillusionment Priestley still hoped to see an Unitarian Society safely founded in America. We may gather from his letters that hope and despair alternated. His first winter in Philadelphia had been marked by crowds, among whom were the first in the State, attending his services. The second winter the novelty wore off and the audience was so inconsiderable that Priestley thought no more good would come that way. Perhaps he was right in believing that the dread of French principles, and his French citizenship militated against his success. Probably some allowance must be made for the fickleness of the multitude, and the general failure, which can be better seen to-day, of rational religion to minister to the emotions of a crowd.

When Priestley again visited Philadelphia he found the Society of 1796 broken up. The yellow fever had carried off several of the most energetic and the most

---

[1] Ibid. ii. 404.

enterprising of the Society's young men. At times he attended other places of worship, for instance, the Old Swede's Church, which still stands in peaceful dignity on the harbour. On Priestley's last visit to Philadelphia he preached 'to a very crowded room', and on the following Sunday administered the Lord's Supper to what was left of the lay Society. A professed minister was needed to make 'the cause more respectable by giving it a head'.[1] But the seed was sown and still grows.

At home, in Northumberland, he tried to start a Society. 'I have divine service every Lord's-day in my own house, which is then open to everybody',[2] he wrote in his letters to its inhabitants. Here again hope and despondency mingled, for on November 6, 1800 he declared he had 'a decent congregation, and a pretty good class of young men'.[3] Six weeks later he regrets that both his 'Congregation and class of young men are something diminished'.[4] At times he lamented that the few Unitarians had not stayed together. William Russell, who, of all others, seemed the most appropriate to settle near Priestley, had perforce to listen to the objections of his family and had gone to Middletown, in Connecticut. And though the law was not enforced against the Russell family, Unitarianism was a crime punishable in the state of Connecticut, in the first instance, with incapacity for office, and the next, with exclusion from the Courts of Law. Priestley considered that this law, though a dead letter, would prevent his settling in the state.[5] During the Adams administration Priestley's position was not enviable and if the law could have been used to annoy him, perhaps some one would have been found ready to set it in motion. Though less pleasantly situated for each other's

[1] Rutt, ii. 506.　　[2] *Works*, xxv.　　[3] Rutt, ii. 445.
[4] Ibid. ii. 449.　　[5] Ibid. ii. 399.

satisfaction, Priestley hoped they would be of greater use 'and a little leaven may in time leaven the whole mass'.[1]

The last ten years of his life were largely given to theological work. Debarred from politics, cut off from philosophical friends except on the rare occasions of his visits to Philadelphia, his first love stood by him till the end. 'I have very little satisfaction', he wrote to Lindsey, 'in any studies that are foreign to this.'[2] His Church History, which, before the Birmingham Riots, had been brought down to the fall of the Western Empire, he now finished, dedicating these last volumes to Jefferson, being desirous because of his long respect for the President 'as a politician and as a man', of connecting his name in some way with that of Jefferson. The actual printing of this work was done at Northumberland under the supervision of Priestley and his son. He was under no anxiety for its outcome, as he could bear the whole expense himself. 'I have no wish', he wrote to Matthew Carey, the Philadelphia bookseller, who had offered to publish the book, 'to gain anything by it, and I do not think I can employ my time, or any money that I can spare, to better purpose than in printing what I have prepared for public use.'[3] In 1799 had appeared *A Comparison of the Institutes of Moses with those of the Hindoos and other ancient Nations,* and his posthumous works included *Notes on all the Books of Scriptures* which fill four of the twenty-five volumes of his works, and *The Doctrines of Heathen Philosophy compared with those of Revelation.* Not content with expounding the scriptures and writing the history of the Church, he set to work to combat infidelity. He thought there was less religion in America than in England. Rational religion, which he believed alone could be

---

[1] Ibid. ii. 440.   [2] Ibid. ii. 387.
[3] Feb. 27th, 1802. 1st Unitarian Church, Philadelphia, MSS.

satisfactorily opposed to infidelity, scarcely existed and while Priestley was preaching and writing against the common enemy, orthodoxy was preaching and writing against him.[1] On his visit to Philadelphia he noted that of those who attended public worship there were 'as many Roman Catholics as of any other persuasion, and that they were not more bigoted than the Presbyterians. The most liberal are the Episcopalians.'[2] With several of these he was very intimate, especially Bishop White, who was orthodox, and Dr. Andrews, who, he declared, was a Unitarian, and who generally came to hear him and who seems to have borne him no ill-will in spite of being a violent Federalist, a pleasing comparison with his friend Dr. Benjamin Rush who, 'though a zealous Christian, and a Unitarian, at least an Arian',[3] never went to hear Priestley. He answered Volney, then a visitor to the United States, and attacked other unbelievers.

It is difficult to be sure how far Priestley really intended to return to Europe. That it was his wish to come back to England or France, so that he might see his friends, is clear after a very casual perusal of the correspondence, and after Mrs. Priestley's death he seems frequently to have played with the idea. Writing to Mrs. Barbauld soon after his wife's death he expressed the desire to see his old friends once more. On April 3rd, 1797, he wrote to Lindsey the decisive news of his return to Europe:

'I am about to go to France, as I see that my property in the French funds will never yield me anything while I remain here, especially as this country is now on bad terms with France. I believe I shall go with the late French ambassador, M. Adet; and Mr. Liston, the English minister, will give me a protection in case of

[1] Rutt, ii. 383.   [2] Ibid. ii. 379.   [3] Ibid. ii. 453.

meeting with an English ship of war. He does the same for M. Adet; so that a better opportunity I could not have had. If I succeed, I shall make some purchase of land in France, and then I can spend my time here or there, as it shall suit me; and, perhaps, I sometimes flatter myself, that having been of some use in promoting the cause of the Gospel here, a door, unseen at present, may, in the course of Providence, be opened for me in France for the same purpose.'[1]

In this letter he directed Lindsey to send his next letter to him at 'M. Perigaux, Banker, in Paris', but the voyage was abandoned, as his son Joseph did not approve. The intention of going to France, however, was not renounced. Apparently Talleyrand had promised to help Priestley should he visit France, and had expressed a hope that they would meet there.

We may believe that Priestley became attached to Northumberland. A line of stage-coaches was operating by 1797 and bridges were being built over the worst creeks, though in 1803 there was still no bridge across the Susquehanna at Northumberland or Sunbury. The crossing was not without danger, and the only whipping the Doctor's grandson remembered getting was in consequence of disobeying his grandfather and crossing the river on foot.[2] In spite of improvements the journey to Philadelphia still took five days at the beginning of the century. A parcel of books sent to the neighbouring town of Carlisle by mistake remained there two years before Priestley received them. The post was but weekly, and Priestley was never sure that it had not been tampered with. English newspapers were few and very often many months overdue.

On his return from Philadelphia in April 1801 he

[1] Ibid. ii. 375.   [2] *Christian Register*, May 7th, 1908.

notes how astonishingly the countryside had improved in the last four years, 'I do not think that any part of England is better cultivated, and at present the wheat is in a very promising state. I wish we may hear of that of England promising as well.'[1] 'Were I to tell you of all the improvements', he wrote to Belsham, 'that have been made in this remote part of the country since our arrival, I might write a little volume, and the amount would hardly appear credible.'[2] One wishes that he had turned aside from theology to carry out this idea.

In the days before the Americans had discovered the way of keeping their houses at perpetual summer heat, the cold in winter must have been intense; yet the amount of sunshine compared very favourably, then as now, with England. 'I have as much *sunshine* as I want, which was far from the case in England',[3] and he assures Belsham that he greatly preferred its climate to England's, 'especially for my experiments, many of which require sunshine, of which I have now plenty; whereas I have watched every gleam in England, and often to no purpose, for months together'.[4]

The last years of his life seem to have been troubled by various complaints. In 1802 he began to be troubled by deafness, and ordered an ear trumpet, but he was thankful that his eyesight remained good. During the summer of 1803 a severe fall on the hip caused him much pain and necessitated the use of crutches, and temporarily cut him off from his laboratory.

The last two visits to Philadelphia, now no longer the seat of government, took place in 1801 and 1803. The first visit was marred by a serious illness which, at one time, caused the doctors to despair of his life. The

---

[1] Priestley to Vaughan from *Journal of Chemical Education*, Feb. 1927.
[2] Rutt, ii. 447.   [3] Ibid. ii. 433.   [4] Ibid. ii. 447.

reason for his last visit was the dislike his son and daughter-in-law had of leaving him behind. He managed to preach to what of the Unitarian Society had survived the yellow fever, and administered to it the Lord's Supper. Much must have been his pleasure at the dinner which the American Philosophical Society gave him.

'Sir': runs the notice, 'You are hereby invited to join the other members of the AMERICAN PHILOSOPHICAL SOCIETY, in giving a testimony of respect, to their venerable associate Dr. JOSEPH PRIESTLEY, who dines with them on Saturday next at Francis' Hotel. Dinner on table at 3 o'clock.

C. Wistar
J. Williams
J. R. Smith ⟩ COMMITTEE
T. T. Hewson
J. Vaughan

'An answer will be called for to-morrow morning.'[1]

Priestley did not fully recover from the illness of 1801. His digestion was impaired, and he could swallow little beyond liquids. Between November 1803 and January his illness grew worse, though he believed he was holding his own, but he was forced to give up taking Divine service, a blow of which the seriousness can only be fully realized when we remember that from his youth up he had put his calling as a Christian Minister before everything. During January he became much weaker; to the very end, on February 6th, he was working, dictating, altering, correcting proofs, &c.

On the evening of the 5th he called his little grand-children to him and exhorted each one separately, 'I am

[1] *Scientific Correspondence*, p. 161.

going to sleep as well as you,' he said,[1] 'for death is only a good long sound sleep in the grave, and we shall meet again.'[2] Death came next day so peacefully and so quietly that neither Joseph nor his wife, who were watching by him, noticed his passing.[3]

[1] Rutt, ii. 530.   [2] Ibid. 530.   [3] Ibid. 531.

EPILOGUE

A NEW century had dawned. How far was it a fulfilment of Priestley's hopes and aspirations? In dogmatic religion it saw the developments of Priestley's methods into the Higher Criticism, but the assault on dogma was carried further and went far to overthrow the cherished opinions of the pioneer. In the religious life of the time the amalgamation of the old Presbyterian chapels into an Unitarian society took place, and the new body, in truly Priestleian spirit, refused the adoption of all creeds, dogmas, and definitions. Under the guidance of such men as Martineau in this country and of Channing in America, it sought to put more weight on the things of the spirit and less on those of the intellect, and remove religious life further from what was often but barren theological discussion. Neither the Anglican nor Roman Catholic Churches proved themselves so near to death and decay as Priestley had believed. Religious tolerance was achieved. In 1812 the Act of William III against non-trinitarians was repealed, and in 1828 the Test and Corporation Acts, and in the following year Catholic Emancipation was carried. Priestley, who had been horrified with the apparent ease with which clergy of the Established Church could sign assent to the truth of articles which they denied in their daily speech, would have seen as the century progressed a vast increase in this evil. Very few, like Stopford Brooke, imitated Theophilus Lindsey, and went out from the church and resigned its emoluments.

The rise of the modern universities filled the need that had been served by the Dissenting academies in the previous century, and had he lived, no doubt Priestley would have supported, along with Campbell, Bentham, and others, the founding of London University.

Priestley's scientific discoveries remain; his theories have vanished. Science to-day claims him as one of her greatest sons.

Priestley was thus eminently a pioneer. He pointed out roads down which others should go. He pressed on further to unexplored regions, leaving them for others to develop. But above all, it was in his life, by his zeal, by his readiness to labour every day, and all day, by his fortitude in the day of trouble, by his undaunted courage in every good cause, that he showed the only way in which work of any value may be achieved, and mankind served.

INDEX